Please remember that this is a library book,
and that it belongs only temporarily to each
person who uses it. Be considerate. Do
not write in this, or any, library book.

Accountability in Education

Philosophy of Education Research Library

Series editors
  V. A. Howard and Israel Scheffler
  Harvard Graduate School of Education

Already published

The Uses of Schooling
  Harry S. Broudy

Educating Reason: Rationality, Critical Thinking and Education
  Harvey Siegel

Thinking in School and Society
  Francis Schrag

Plato's Metaphysics of Education
  Samuel Scolnicov

The Sense of Art: A Study in Aesthetic Education
  Ralph A. Smith

The Teacher: Theory and Practice in Education
  Allen Pearson

Liberal Justice and the Marxist Critique of Education
  Kenneth A. Strike

Accountability in Education:

A Philosophical Inquiry

Robert B. Wagner

Routledge

New York   London

First published in 1989 by
Routledge
an imprint of Routledge, Chapman & Hall, Inc.
29 West 35th Street
New York NY 10001

Published in Great Britain by
Routledge
11 New Fetter Lane
London EC4P 4EE

© *1989 by Routledge, Chapman and Hall*

Printed in the United States of America

Library of Congress Cataloging in Publication Data

Wagner, Robert B., 1937–
    Accountability in education : a philosophical inquiry / Robert B.
  Wagner.
       p.   cm.—(The Philosophy of education research library)
    Bibliography: p.
    Includes index.
    ISBN 0–415–90091–3
    1. Educational accountability—United States.   I. Title.
II. Series.
LB2806.22.W34   1989
379.1'54—dc20   89–35569
                                               CIP

British Library Cataloguing in Publication Data also available.

TO
C.W.G. AND R.J.F.
teachers—mentors—friends

Contents

Introduction

Major institutions and organizations are frequently criticized for engaging in practices which appear to be self-serving and contrary to the public interest, or for pursuing ends that are outdated or at least misguided in terms of their primary purpose. Critics allege that both problems are serious because they involve processes in which institutions become increasingly insensitive to the needs of the very groups they were intended to serve. Two observations are worth noting. First, these criticisms became especially focused as public issues during the 1960s and 1970s. While it is true that those who voice them today may be less strident in promoting their concerns, the basic criticisms remain and are directed at rather diverse institutions in both the public and private sectors of this society, e.g., social service agencies, business and corporate industry, medicine, and education, as well as judicial, legislative and executive branches at all levels of government. Second, these criticisms often involve the position that if these same institutions were less autonomous and more "accountable" greater harmony between their performance and the public interest would be assured.

Public education offers an illustration. Past and present criticisms of education have a striking similarity and involve fundamental issues and problems ranging from educational purpose, procedures and reform to questions of accessibility and whether the results of education justify related expenditures. In the midst of the continuing controversy over these issues there has been a persistent belief that these problems could be resolved or at least better managed if the nation's schools and those who teach in them were more "accountable." Whether or not this belief and the assumptions about education which generally attend it are valid is a concern of this study. But of greater concern is the degree to which proposals for accountability often fail to recognize basic elements and conditions of this concept or fail to consider the full range of its implications. For example, to contend that an individual or an institution ought to be accountable immediately brings to mind the questions: accountable to whom, for what, in what manner and under what circumstances?

Articles have appeared in the literature for a number of years attempting to answer these questions and to offer proposals for accountability designed to improve education, but interpretations of this concept remain ambiguous and a conceptual framework has yet to evolve which deals adequately with its constituent elements and ethical dimensions. In response, accountability proponents could argue that despite various and sometimes conflicting interpretations of accountability there is at least general agreement about the following: (1) The quality of schools can no longer be determined simply by looking at input factors such as plant facilities, the number of volumes in the library, pupil/teacher ratios or printed curricula; rather, school performance and the quality of school programs are best understood in terms of results and output, what children do or do not learn over a given period; (2) learning can be measured against costs for a specified interval as an indication of cost-effectiveness; (3) taxpayers, parents and supportive government agencies have a "right" to know about these results and the cost/benefits associated with their schools; and (4) accountability can provide this information and act as a stimulus to better school performance.

These assumptions do have a certain appeal. To maintain that those who support the costs of education are entitled to an accounting of how their money is spent and the benefits derived from such expenditure seems reasonable, and a closer look at the "results" of schooling may be a consideration too long ignored. However, not all that appears reasonable proves to be so upon closer examination. Many proposals for accountability focus on the accountability of teachers because they assume that teachers are responsible for student performance and ultimately for what students learn or fail to learn as a result of their classroom experience. But several assumptions offered in support of this position require further consideration and careful analysis. For example, is responsibility for learning an exclusive responsibility? Do parents and other groups bear any responsibility for the experiences that children have while they are in school? To what extent are students responsible for what they learn or fail to learn? Should they be held accountable for learning as well as behavior, and if so, what approaches should be adopted regarding their accountability?

The present study has been undertaken in the belief that before "accountability" can be effectively implemented as an institutional or personal requirement, a reasonable understanding of its conceptual dimensions must be acquired; that such understanding is now lacking; and that this contention is supported by applications of this concept in a number of fields. Specifically:

1. What does it mean to be accountable?
2. Are there principles and considerations of a general sort that ought to govern various applications of this concept and the relationships they involve?
3. What conditions must be present on any occasion to justify a demand for accountability or its expectation, to justify the requirements it may impose and, once justified, provide assurance that these requirements will be satisfied?

4. Are there degrees or levels of accountability, and if so, what factors are most influential in determining the degree of accountability that will exist on any given occasion and within agent relationships involving this concept?

To arrive at answers to these questions, several terms will be analyzed which are considered to be either definitive of or synonymous with the term *accountability*. This analysis will establish that the concepts of "obligation", "responsibility" and "entitlement" are highly relevant to any accountability relationship and that several factors influence the nature and efficacy of such relationships when they occur.

As the central features of accountability are explored and developed in this study, many examples will be drawn from education, business, law and practical experience to illustrate points that must be made about this concept and to provide a basis for discussion. But the study itself is primarily a philosophical analysis with the objectives of determining the central features of accountability, its role and justification as a personal and institutional requirement, and how it relates to selected problems in the field of education. A number of articles and several books appeared throughout the seventies, when the accountability movement in education gained considerable momentum. The rationale and assumptions behind this movement were largely established and articulated then; consequently, several writings from this period will be considered in the discussion to assist the overall analysis and general argument presented.

In completing this study I owe much to Israel Scheffler and Vernon Howard. I am indebted to Israel Scheffler not only for his teaching, but also because he provided studies in the philosophy of education that were academically sound and which for me were very meaningful. They altered the way in which I view my profession as an educator, and they changed the manner in which I approach the problems and issues associated with it. I am grateful to Vernon Howard because of his longstanding belief that accountability is an important concept in our lives, and for his patience and encouragement throughout the process of completing this manuscript.

Accountability is an interesting subject because it is such a pervasive feature in many of the relationships that occur in human affairs. There are important questions that need to be addressed about this concept and its application within a number of fields and professions. The following discussion will not answer all of these questions, but it will identify several issues and considerations that should be of value to those who wish to explore them.

PART I

Forms of accounting

CHAPTER 1

Accounting to others and being answerable

The term *accountability*

The concept of "accountability" and its implications are quite complex from both a theoretical and a practical standpoint. This complexity may be partly due to the term's origins, for even a brief review of its etymology reveals considerable variation in meaning among antecedent terms from which it evolved. *Accountability* and the adjective *accountable* ultimately derive from the verb *account,* which in its earliest usage meant literally "to reckon, count, count up or calculate," as, for example, in the sentence "A bank clerk should be able to account."[1] The definition "to render an account of, to explain and to answer for" came into use between the early and late 1600s.

As one might expect, there are a number of similarities between the verb *account* and the meanings which have evolved during the development of its substantive form. In the latter function it has been used to imply: counting, calculating or reckoning, as in "He is quick at accounts" (Middle English); a statement of monies received and paid, a reckoning in one's favor or to one's advantage, as in "to do something for one's own account"(1611). By 1614 the term could be used to mean a report, relation or description, such as providing an account of one's trip or an incident. Many of these meanings occur in a contemporary usage that continues to expand.[2] According to one authority, account can now imply "a statement of explanation of one's conduct; a statement or exposition of reasons, causes, grounds, or motives"; and, as a verb, to furnish a justifying analysis. In addition, the term *accountable* can be used to imply being "obligated to give an account" or being "subject" to doing so.[3]

There are several preliminary comments to be made concerning these definitions. The first relates to Wittgenstein's observation that the uses of a term are often extensive, and in some cases so extensive as to preclude formulating any definition that would be capable of conveying the full range of the term's meaning. According to Wittgenstein, such uses actually comprise a "family" of meanings in the sense that they are united "by a complicated network of similarities overlapping and crisscrossing; sometimes similarities of a general nature; in some cases, similarities of detail."[4]

It is equally characteristic of many terms that in spite of the similarities which seem to unify their various meanings, certain of these meanings are obvious in their departure from the term's more central uses. The word *run* offers a good example. We speak of a person running down the street, a candidate running for office; remark that a machine is running or that a highway runs through a particular town. Though related, each of these expressions is used to convey a meaning unique in its own intention. The notion of a highway running through town is a more peripheral use of the term than that in which the idea of someone literally running is intended, even though the idea of motion or something going someplace may be brought to mind in both instances.

Several meanings presented for the term *account* have these features. Among them one is able to discover similarities: Giving an account of monies received and paid, in one sense a report of such transactions, seems analogous to the idea of providing an account of what has occurred during an event or giving a report on matters transpiring over a period of time. However, more noticeable differences in connotation also occur: to use *account* for purposes of implying that one is quick at counting or calculation is quite different from implying that one is to provide some form of explanation. Therefore, our first point is that the terms *account* and *accountability* share an important feature with other general terms: In no way can we formulate a single definition and maintain that this is what giving an account really means or find a definition to convey all that would be implied by an adequate concept or theory of accountability.

From the above we should not conclude that definitions are useless or that they lack value in language; on the contrary, a basic function of definitions is not to convey the full meaning of a term but to delimit and thereby confine its implication to what is intended on the particular occasion of its usage. While it is true that an adequate concept of accountability would necessarily include features impossible to convey by definitions, the preceding definitions do represent standard usage and to this extent are at least indicative of what might be intended whenever it is alleged that a particular person or institution ought to be accountable. For this reason, an analysis of several of these meanings can be of value in promoting an understanding of various features of a concept that each alone fails to encompass.

Giving an account

If it is fairly representative of standard usage to hold that being accountable means, among other things, being obligated or subject to giving account, then in saying that a particular agent is accountable we could imply that he is obligated to give a report, relation, description, explanation, justifying analysis, or some form of exposition[5] for we have observed that from an etymological standpoint the term *account* has come to mean each of the above. These terms and the forms of accounting they represent belong to the same "family" of meanings and share certain connotative similarities; however, it is not at all clear that they are synonymous in either the requirements they impose on an accountant or the kinds of considerations that may be relevant to their satisfaction. For example, school administrators are occasionally required to report on the distribution of funds for various school programs and on the expenditure of such funds throughout the fiscal year. This type of accounting seems different from a situation in which the administrator is expected to explain or to justify why certain funds were allocated as they were, or why they were or were not expended in a particular manner.

Cases involving disclosure also illustrate this distinction. Suppose a candidate for political office is considered morally and legally accountable to "the people" regarding the nature of his campaign contributions. He might be expected to make such information a matter of public record; to periodically state or publish the names of contributors and the amounts of their contributions. Being obligated to give this form of account, and nothing more, seems different in its requirement than having to face a congressional subcommittee or the public via the media to *justify* why certain amounts were accepted or were accepted from certain parties.

Similarly, if a person is obligated to give a routine accounting of his financial affairs, through use of a standard income tax form, something different is involved than if he is subsequently called upon to explain or justify these affairs or the manner in which they may have been reported. In the first instance in each of these cases, the party in question is simply requested to file a report, presumed to be factual by virtue of summarizing events that actually occurred. In the second instance, the school administrator, politician and taxpayer are required to go beyond the mere reporting of certain events and explain *why* they occurred as they did or were reported as they were. What must be provided, and what eventually may be called into question, are the grounds, motives, or reasons prompting whatever actions their reports truly represent, though perhaps intentionally or unintentionally obscure. In each of these cases, then, circumstances attending the second instance of accountability have varied in an important respect; for they involve expectations which can be satisfied neither by the same considerations nor by the same form of accounting required in the first instance.

Now in making the distinction between *reporting* the constituent elements of an event and *explaining* or *justifying* their occurrence, we do not wish to deny that an appeal to fact will often be made when offering an explanation or justification of something, such as stating a motive or reason that played a role in the matter. The taxpayer in this case might say that he failed to declare certain income for reason of extreme hardship or oversight, and his statement could be factual; but what is important from the standpoint of accountability is that his statement is given because it is relevant to a justification of his original actions. Determining guilt or deciding whether he was right or wrong under the circumstances each would require an appeal to considerations other than simply what he did or did not do, e.g. reference to law, accepted moral principles or knowledge of human behavior by which the validity of whatever argument he presents in his defense may be ascertained. We might fully acknowledge that our taxpayer broke the law by falsifying his original account, recognize the punishment prescribed for this offense and yet still believe that other extenuating factors ought to be taken into consideration, e.g. his state of mind or the fact of extreme hardship together with the moral obligation to provide for one's family.

For the present, whether the reasons given correspond to fact or whether they should be accepted as sufficient justification for his original actions is not of primary concern. What is to be emphasized is that the distinction between reporting what has occurred and attempting to explain or justify the "why" of its occurrence is central in human affairs. In law, witnesses are instructed to present only the facts; to relate in their account only what was seen or heard and not to offer explanations or suppositions that are essentially the prerogative of others. It is true that in a particular case experts may be called upon to offer hypotheses in its regard, but usually such testimony is designated for what it is and the person testifying must provide, within his analytical account, some justification for his conclusions.

The fact that these distinctions are critical in many spheres of human interest is evident in the consultant role which lawyers, doctors, scientists and other professionals are asked to fulfill because of their specialized knowledge and expertise. It is one thing to relate that an individual has behaved in a particular way and quite another to explain his behavior; one thing to describe current economic conditions and state why they exist, or to report that one has followed a given course of action, and another to justify that course of action. These forms of accounting are unique not only because of what they require from an accountant, but also because of the kind of information and the degree of insight they will yield about any given phenomenon.

It is necessary to deal with two criticisms that could be raised about these distinctions. The first would allege that frequently they are nonexistent; that on numerous occasions the requirements imposed by various forms of accounting and the considerations which may be necessary for their satisfaction are very similar or difficult to discern; that in science, for example, this is especially true where a report or description of research often involves explanation and thus brings together the elements of both narrative description and explanatory analysis, and may even include justifying assumptions or setting forth causes or reasons.

I think we can acknowledge this criticism and yet maintain the foregoing distinctions. It is true that in giving a report, a scientist could say that he observed x, y, and z, and that in his judgment z resulted from a conjunction of x and y for certain reasons. But this only means that an explanation of something can be presented in a narrative report. By no means does this alter the fact that an explanation had to be formulated at some point and, once formulated, becomes a matter of fact capable of being reported like any other. It therefore does not negate the distinction that must be made among: (1) reporting that x, y, and z have occurred; (2) offering an explanation as to the "why" of their occurrence; and (3) subsequently justifying the position taken. [6]

The second criticism recognizes these distinctions, but maintains that calling attention to them is trivial because they are obvious. However obvious they may be, the distinctions themselves are not trivial from the standpoint of accountability. Consider the case of the high school teacher who observes the physical assault of one student upon another, then intervenes and in the process strikes one of the students, ostensibly in self-defense. Undoubtedly, the teacher in question would be expected to make a report, that is, to give an account of what happened. In reporting the incident the teacher very likely would be expected to justify his actions in striking the student. Should his conduct be called into question, his vulnerability to civil suit and perhaps his very ability to retain his position could depend on the adequacy of his explanation and the kinds of argument and reasons he brings forth to justify his actions. Individuals who have been in the position of having to explain or to justify a matter of personal importance should grasp the conceptual point we are making about these forms of accounting and the distinctions among them. But does the mere act of explaining or justifying something in itself exhaust and fully comprehend all that is implied by the concept of "accountability" or for that matter "being accountable"? This is doubtful when another interpretation is examined.

Being answerable

If in saying "X is accountable to Y for Z" we mean "X is answerable to Y for Z" we could imply (a) that X is to give some type of answer to Y similar to those discussed, in which case being "answerable" would be analogous to giving "an account"; or (b) that X is to answer to Y for Z in some sense other than giving an account.

Several examples have been presented to illustrate the first implication; however, the second raises the question: Under what condition is it justifiable to say that an agent *has been* accountable? Consider the case of a manufacturing concern X, responsible for marketing a product containing a toxic substance Z. Should death or injury occur attributable to the product, it is conceivable that a suit or some form of litigation might ensue. Under the previous interpretation of accountability, if X is obligated to give an explanation of its actions and does so in its defense, one could say that it *has been* accountable to the extent of having given an account of its responsibility in the matter. But more could be expected. Damages could be claimed and awarded to a plaintiff Y. In paying a settlement, is X answering to Y for Z?

The situation of our taxpayer is similar. If he submits a report to the government concerning his income it is clear that he has given an account; and if the report is satisfactory it would seem that in this instance he has been accountable, that he *has been* answerable for his financial affairs in a manner falling under interpretation (a). But if his report proves unacceptable and a penalty is imposed, it seems correct to say that his accountability was not concluded, since he now must answer further in a manner under interpretation (b). Demand for restitution and assignment of punishment are important elements in law. In judicial matters it is established practice to hold either that persons who violate certain laws incur a debt to society, or that having to answer for what they have done through some form of punishment will serve to prevent similar violations on the part of others. If this is recognized, then the notion of "being answerable" for something is more extensive and represents an additional form of accounting, one which can be more exacting in its requirements.

Degree of accountability: first analysis

The foregoing distinctions suggest a further possibility. If the forms of accounting one might be obligated to give do differ in (1) the requirements they impose on an individual or institution and (2) the considerations necessary for their satisfaction, it might be appropriate to think of varying degrees of accountability depending on the type of account expected and the requirements involved. Should the expected form of account be such that (1) and (2) are easily satisfied, a relatively low degree of accountability could be said to exist; whereas if the expected account imposes more stringent requirements, a higher degree of accountability would be operative.

A number of illustrations presented thus far lend credibility to this notion. Generally speaking, reporting one's financial affairs by means of a tax statement is a requirement more easily satisfied and therefore a lower degree of accountability than being subject to some form of penalty or having to present a justification in their regard. Similarly, if a candidate for office is considered accountable for campaign contributions, having to face a subcommittee or the public to justify why certain contributions were accepted seems a more exacting and perhaps revealing form of accountability than a routine disclosure statement. The original disclosure would be a form of accountability, to be sure, but it is, nevertheless, a weaker form of accounting than the second.[7]

But is the degree of accountability operating in any given situation solely a function of the requirements which happen to be imposed on the agent? Do we wish to maintain that persons subject to providing a justification are *ipso facto* always more accountable, that is, subject to a greater degree of accountability, than persons who are simply required to report or to describe a given matter? Figure 1.1 presents these factor relationships by means of four quadrants into which various cases of accountability could be assigned. If we do make the preceding assumption, several cases can be explained which fall into quadrants 2 and 3.

For example, 2 would include those cases where the expectation is for an explanation, justification or penalty, the requirements are more difficult to satisfy, and the agent's accountability would be greater. Quadrant 3 would include cases where something is related or a report is expected, less stringent requirements are involved, and a lower degree of accountability seems operative. According to this analysis, filling out an income tax statement falls somewhere in quadrant 3, as would making a nonexplanatory statement about campaign contributions, or issuing a financial statement concerning school budget expenditures; whereas quadrant 2 would most appropriately describe having to offer a justifying analysis of such matters, or the more stringent forms of being answerable represented by penalties or making restitution.

But does a theory of covarience involving only these two factors adequately explain the degree of accountability that could be operative in all situations? This is doubtful if one examines the variable relationships descriptive of quadrants 1 and 4. In quadrant 4 we have those cases involving less severe requirements due to a nonexplanatory form of accounting, and yet we would wish to say that a fairly *high* degree of accountability exists. Quadrant 1 would include cases in which the expected form of account does impose greater requirements, yet the degree of accountability seems *low*. Two questions must be pursued concerning this model. First, do any cases of accountability fall into quadrants 1 and 4; if so, a covarience theory involving only factor A would be insufficient. Second, if this theory is insufficient and the degree of accountability is determined by other factors, either in conjunction with A or independently, what might they be?

Regarding the first question, it can be demonstrated that certain cases do occur and would be more correctly described by quadrants 1 and 4. Though a distinction was made between reporting and justifying one's financial affairs to some agency of the government, both differ from a situation in which the party in question offers similar accounts to a friend relative or even his lawyer. What can differ in these examples is not only the form of account presented, but to whom it is given and whether the agent is "obligated to" give it. In the first instance he is required to file a tax statement; if he refuses or his report

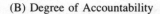

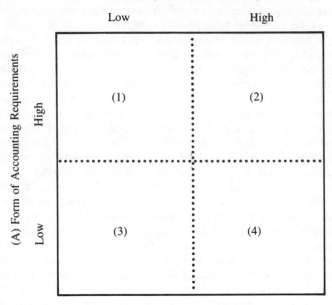

Figure 1.1

proves unsatisfactory, the possibility remains that the matter will be pursued further, irrespective of his wishes. In the second example of explaining or trying to justify his financial affairs to a friend or relative, this possibility is nonexistent or at least far more remote.

Two elements are conjoined in the second term of the proposition "X is accountable means that X is obligated to give an account." They are "giving an account" *and* being "obligated" to give it. It is doubtful whether the mere provision of an account would be sufficient grounds for saying that an agent is accountable or has been accountable. As we have noted, individuals frequently relate, explain or attempt to justify something they have done, experienced or hope to do, and in circumstances in which the element of their being "subject to" doing so does not always feature; circumstances in which giving an account is largely a matter of personal choice. Quadrant 1 represents those cases where a fairly difficult form of account is involved, but the agent providing it has this discretion; we would not say the same for cases included in quadrant 4 because the degree of freedom or personal choice in the matter is far less, even though the expected form of account may impose requirements more easily satisfied.

In regard to the two questions posed above, then, it is reasonable to conclude (a) that while various *forms* of accounting may involve requirements and reveal information influencing the degree of account-ability in any given situation, cases appropriate to quadrants 1 and 4 also occur suggesting the relevance of other factors; and (b) that, seemingly, one such factor is whether the agent is "obligated" to give the account. Unfortunately, this raises more questions than it answers. First, if the element of obligation is a necessary condition of accountability, then under circumstances in which one is warranted in saying "X is account-able," which becomes more significant to the degree of accountability involved: (1) the form of account expected; (2) the basis or grounds on which X is obligated to give it; or (3) some further possibility?

Second, our remarks to this point suggest that if the privilege of refusing to give an account is absent, it is absent because in some sense the agent is "obligated" to give it. But in what sense? What could be the source and nature of such an obligation? What we wish to find out is simpler to state than to determine. If an agent in the course of his relations with others can become obligated to give an account or to be answerable in any of the forms previously discussed, what factors estab-lish such a position, or more importantly, should establish it? In part II of this study, the conditions which validate obligations of accountability and constitute the basis for accountability relationships will be examined; special attention will be given to the problems of agent compliance and other factors which may have a bearing on the degree of accountability operating in such relationships. But additional groundwork must be provided before these issues can be approached in a sensible discussion. For the present, two related topics of concern require our attention in the remainder of this chapter and the chapter which follows.

The first involves the forms or various methods of accounting pre-viously discussed. From an empirical standpoint, people spend much of their time accounting to others; they relate, explain or attempt to justify a seemingly endless number of matters involving their personal and professional lives. As an essential element of communication, these forms of accounting are a constant and pervasive feature in human relationships, and the field of education is no exception. In the daily course of teaching and operating a school, teachers and administrators frequently report on student progress and explain budgets and curricula; they must justify school policies and in one form or another account to superiors, parents and various constituencies within the community. Moreover, throughout the course of their schooling we expect students to describe events, to analyze and explain problems, and to justify and offer supporting arguments for the theories and positions they advance; in essence, they must provide written and oral accounts concerning behavior and what they are expected to learn. Whether the matter is important or relatively insignificant, in each of these transactions one agent or party is providing some form of accounting to another. Examples have been presented to illustrate the distinctions among these forms of accounting and the fact that they are necessarily required in daily communication and in the life of a school; but if they represent a primary element of accountability, as we have argued, further consideration must be given to their function and what it ought to be in the context of education, especially where demands for greater accountability have the potential of being articulated in practices that may adversely affect the learning of students or the professional work of their teachers. Is it possible to expect forms of accounting that are unfair from the standpoint of those who must provide them, to implement accountability arrangements that are inconsistent with the aims of education or which have little value because they fail to serve either the purposes for which they were designed or purposes that are educationally sound? These possibilities exist and the problems they pose do occur, which brings us to a second related topic.

Although the preceding forms of accounting are as common in education as they are in other areas of social activity, it is clear from the history of the accountability movement that numerous people find traditional arrangements for educational accountability inadequate and to an extent that justifies reform. Their concern has been accompanied by a variety of proposals to address the issue. Exploring the assumptions of this movement and the proposals that have grown from it will quickly demonstrate that accountability is a concept with complex dimensions from both an ethical and a practical point of view, and will reveal several issues that must be considered in contexts wherever this concept is applied. Identifying these issues will further our understanding of accountability generally, but it also will put us in a better position to frame principles and strategies for accountability consistent with the aims of education and the responsibilities that students and educators must fulfill.

The demand for accountability in education

In June 1985, at the annual convention of the National Education Association, seventy-five hundred delegates gave overwhelming approval to resolutions which endorsed licensing examinations for new teachers and the dismissal of experienced teachers found to be incompetent. Both resolutions were introduced by an NEA leadership whose predecessors had long opposed such measures, and in this respect their passage represented a victory for supporters of an accountability movement that really began in the seventies. The earlier pressure for educational accountability had provoked controversy and major initiatives to alter public policy in a number of states, but the emergence of this movement can be traced to three basic concerns which remain today and comprise a major component of the rationale behind the demand for greater accountability in education.

One involves concern over rising costs in public services, which are extensive today and each year claim a greater amount of personal income through taxation. Since the mid-seventies, public opinion polls and voter behavior reveal closer scrutiny on the part of taxpayers who are no longer satisfied with knowing the qualifications of teachers, whether schools have the latest facilities and equipment, or even how much a given budget will be, but to an unprecedented extent press for a reduction in school costs, reject budget proposals outright and demand that schools and teachers be held accountable for greater effectiveness, especially when increased funding is requested.[8]

Concern over rising costs and whether they are justified by educational outcomes has been evident at the federal level as well, especially during the years immediately following the Johnson administration. Former associates and spokespersons for the Office of Education, administering programs through subordinate offices such as the Office of Educational Opportunity, (OEO) contended that massive sums of money were made available to the schools through various titles under the Defense and Elementary-Secondary Education Acts, with little provision for effectively demonstrating the achievement of the goals they were intended to support; and that it would be unrealistic to expect federal spending to continue at this level, let alone increase, without some evidence of the results obtained.[9]

The second development is closely related and involves a fundamental criticism that is voiced as much today as in the past; namely, that schools are failing unacceptable numbers of youths. It is argued that the dropout rate continues to be high, involving one in every four students, and that a similar number have been found to be functionally illiterate when applying for jobs and induction into the armed services, unable to perform even the most elementary computation. Lessinger, a leading proponent of accountability, called attention to the problem during the seventies.

> If one airplane in every four crashed between takeoff and landing, people would refuse to fly. If one automobile in every four went out of control and caused a fatal accident or permanent injury, Detroit would be closed down tomorrow. Our schools—which produce a more important product than air-planes or automobiles—somehow fail one youngster in four. And so far we have not succeeded in preventing the social and economic fatalities every school dropout represents.[10]

However, Lessinger's comment points to another trend in this movement: the frequent use of modern business as an ideal model for school management and accountability.

Education and the business metaphor

Proponents of the business model argue that by utilizing engineering and management techniques long known to business, and to which much of its success may be attributed, education can overcome serious problems of inefficiency and economy.

> In essence, these procedures that have worked well in certain areas emphasize: clarifying goals, designing plans for attaining them, measuring progress toward them, diagnosing difficulties, and redesigning the plan, with subsequent appraisal, and further revisions, if necessary. In applying strategic planning, the total organization and its several parts are held accountable for reaching the goals. As these management procedures are becoming more widely known, they are frequently being recommended by businessmen and other laymen for use in schools.[11]

Other techniques cited as possible innovation include systems analysis, contract engineering, logistics, value and human-factors engineering, and programs for quality assurance which approximate the "zero defect" concept in aerospace industries.

> If to these are added instructional technology and modern educational management theory, a new valuable interdisciplinary field emerges. This body of knowledge, skill and procedure can be called educational engineering. It is the insights from educational engineering that make it possible for performance contracting to achieve accountability for results in education.[12]

Though the "product" of schools is usually stated to be more important, it is clear from much of their writing that accountability proponents consider business to be more successful in achieving efficiency, economy and results, which they attribute to rather sophisticated procedures that should now be employed in education. The basic argument can be summarized as follows:

A. Education must contend with three serious problems:
   1. rising costs;
   2. a significant incidence of failure in achieving results, particularly in basic skills, which represents waste in terms of dollars spent; and,
   3. growing demands for accountability which appear justified in view of 1 and 2.
B. This needed accountability can effectively counter each of the above if it incorporates the managerial and engineering techniques of modern business that have accounted for the greater success of business in achieving results and efficiency of operation.

That the preceding assumptions have influenced the accountability movement and underlie much of the rationale behind it is undeniable; but it is one thing to recognize that certain developments have contributed to this movement and quite another to infer that because they exist various demands for accountability or particular conceptions of it are fully justified. These inferences are frequently drawn, but are subject to three major criticisms: one is that those who point to taxpayer concern, school failure and the success of business in their arguments for accountability seldom question general or personal assumptions about each of these developments; the second has to do with the fact that most proposals for accountability rest on the belief that business and education are sufficiently comparable to use similar accountability procedures; the third involves the general tendency in these proposals to ignore the ethical considerations which any application of this concept requires. In our view, the second and third are more serious limitations and will occupy our attention in the remaining chapters, but the first criticism deserves passing comment before they are examined.

Assumptions concerning costs and efficiency

It is true that costs in education have risen sharply; the trend began in the postwar period and continues today.[13] But its earlier advance was partly due to a rapidly growing population which expected public education to be extended to all, creating demands for additional facilities, programs, and personnel. Moreover, the late fifties and sixties were a period of greater attention to the special needs of children. Many school systems implemented programs in speech therapy, remedial reading, and health services, expanded the functions of guidance and counseling, and tried newer approaches to vocational training and the education of slow-learning and neurologically impaired youths.[14] It would be logically inconsistent for a society to sharply increase its birthrate, expect to extend and expand its educational services to the larger clientele it has produced, and at the same time not to expect school costs to rise dramatically.

Some may object that agitation over school costs did not occur during the period when schools enjoyed considerable public support; that the concern has arisen, when costs in education continue to rise despite a declining birthrate. It is obvious that the special programs mentioned above would not have developed without the necessary support for them; and the effect of Sputnik on our willingness to increase spending in the sciences during the fifties is now legend. But what this view overlooks is the fact that as newer services are introduced, this invariably establishes a broader cost base, subject to factors of inflation not uncommon to other areas of the economy, especially when programs are maintained over a period of years. Is there any reason to assume that construction, maintenance and operating costs should be substantially less in education or immune to the economic contingencies affecting most institutions? A basic question to be asked is whether educational costs are growing at a rate which compares unfavorably with other sectors of the economy; and if so, whether there are reasons to justify them.

Proponents of educational accountability frequently refer to defense and aerospace programs in presenting examples of efficiency and productivity, but fail to mention the excessive cost overruns tolerated in these industries.[15] Considerable sums were spent in developing prototypes such as the SST and F-111 aircraft, only to find them unusable, unsatisfactory or involving costs far in excess of those originally proposed. Inadequate mechanisms for accountability in these industries can result in the loss of life, a fact quite evident in this nation's space shuttle disaster. If the issue is accountability for money spent, how much does the American public know about defense or government spending in general—the cost/benefit involved—or the consumer about cost/profit ratios determining the price of oil to heat his home or the public utility services on which he is totally dependent? To what extent are inefficiency, costly errors, waste or unjustifiable profit margins covered and passed along to consumers in higher prices; or prices themselves held to competitive levels by cheaper materials and sacrifice of product quality?

Of the expenses eroding personal income today, school costs are probably the most accessible in terms of the average person's either knowing what they are or being able to do anything about them. Taxpayers do not vote directly on the cost of food, shelter, appliances, the family automobile, or for that matter feel they have very much to say about federal taxes,[16] but they often vote on operating and capital improvement levies for schools. To what extent, then, might specific concern over school costs reflect a broader dissatisfaction with today's cost of living, a dissatisfaction which many feel powerless to remedy except through the schools, which are more directly subject to public actions? There is an implicit assumption here that schools have not been accountable when in fact they probably provide more readily available information on costs and answer more directly for them to the public than is true of either business or government.

Advocates of accountability are correct bringing the concern over rising costs to our attention, for this concern is bound to have implications for education in the near and distant future; but if it is to be used as an argument for accountability, some attention ought to be given to whether a number of beliefs and assumptions behind it are justified.

Assumptions about performance

Much the same can be said of the flat assertion that schools fail one of every four students and that greater accountability for results is necessary if this problem is to be overcome. The obvious presumption here is that this failure is entirely the school's, that it is within the ability of teachers and the schools to correct, and that its causes are sufficiently understood to say that accountability, patterned after modern business practice, is the answer. But in the absence of any supporting evidence or analysis, how meaningful is this accusation? Using these same figures, three out of four students today do complete their schooling. How do present figures relating to illiteracy and early termination compare with those over the last fifty years? If three out of four children complete their public schooling today, how many eventually assume positions in the very businesses and industries with which their schools are compared? Just where did the men and women who have contributed to the success of American business receive their education? It is unfortunate that one in every four youngsters fails to complete school, and efforts should be made to remedy this problem, but in much of the writing in which a need for accountability is argued there is a tendency to move too directly from recognition of a genuine problem to its solution, with little intervening consideration of its possible causes—an approach which is, at best, superficial. What factors influence the probability of a child's success in school? Which among these factors can be influenced by the school and which cannot because they involve considerations that are beyond it? In essence, how complex are these problems and will their solution require a more comprehensive approach than seems to be suggested by the notion that accountability or prevailing interpretations of it are the answer?

Assumptions concerning business

If business is the model after which educational accountability should be fashioned, it seems reasonable to ask whether basic assumptions about this model are correct and whether the analogy is fitting. For example, have the engineering and management techniques which are to provide greater accountability in education really done the same in the businesses and industries from which they are taken? The consumer and ecology movements in this country suggest that they have not; for each attests to the fact that throughout the seventies and eighties more and more people became increasingly dissatisfied with many results in business, believing that only measures external to it could remedy such perceived problems as defective consumer goods, price fixing, dishonesty in advertising, exploitation of resources, the illegal use of corporate profits in politics and unreasonable price increases.

One in four automobiles produced in this country may not contribute to death or injury, but enough have done so to cause unprecedented callbacks because of faulty design or workmanship, a practice which became far more noticeable after stronger consumer advocacy in the seventies. Who knows how many deaths or injuries occur through product malfunction, improper design or defective materials—or, of those which do, how many could be prevented with better safety standards? Investigation of safety in children's toys and nonflammable clothing material strongly suggested a need for more information and a greater degree of monitoring in these areas.[17] Undoubtedly, schools can benefit from a number of business procedures, and we shall argue that accountability does have an important role in education; but when it is alleged that business is more successful because it incorporates greater accountability for results, it should be made clear in what respect it is successful and for which results it is accountable.

In presenting their rationale for educational accountability, proponents of this concept frequently offer little evidence to support several key premises on which it rests; and in advocating business as an ideal model they have ignored the fact that demands for accountability today are by no means limited to education, but increasingly are directed at the very businesses they contend it should emulate. It is difficult to see why the same techniques which have failed to provide accountability for many "results" in modern business are assumed to be appropriate for this purpose in education. We shall evaluate this assumption in the next chapter by examining the aims of education in relation to the kinds of results for which schools and teachers are expected to be accountable. Our analysis of the issues raised there will enable us to complete the necessary background for our discussion in part II, but it also will illustrate several problems that can occur when proposals for accountability ignore what the elements of this concept require in accountability relationships, or fail to observe the ethical and logical conditions of accountability which must be recognized if such relationships are to be fair and effective and in the end serve any meaningful purpose.

CHAPTER 2

Accountability and the aims of education

As presently used in the literature, the term *results* closely parallels what is generally meant when one speaks of educational "ends" or "outcomes," and these terms are frequently used interchangeably in discussions of educational accountability. Each can be employed in a prescriptive sense to suggest a preferred state, the ultimate aims or objectives that schools ought to pursue with children, or they can be used descriptively in reference to what actually has or has not been achieved. When accountability proponents argue that teachers should be accountable for "results," their primary concern is with the actual outcomes of education as evidenced by student performance, but it is clear that an assessment concerning the merit of such results presupposes an element of normative judgment; that is, preconceptions of what these results ought to be or ought to have been which serve as criteria in relation to which actual outcomes can be measured.

Of the various forms of accountability proposed for education, the concept of "performance contracting" is often cited as the most effective strategy to assure "accountability for results," and because this concept will enable us to illustrate various problems and issues relating to accountability, it is the interpretation that will occupy our attention in the present and subsequent chapters. Contracts are essentially agreements in which one party promises to render goods, services, or particular results to another for some consideration of value, which the second promises to give in return once the service has been provided. Consequently, the promises involved in a contract are mutually binding and of central importance to a relationship which often involves some manner of redress for nonfulfillment on either side.

Because of their value in delineating the conditions attending agreements and in securing fulfillment of the obligations they entail, formal contracts play a primary role in business and other social relationships and understandably define many agreements in education. Schools frequently contract for building construction, maintenance, student transportation, food services, and for a variety of professional services in which personnel agree to perform specific duties within a given period of time for a fixed remuneration. However, while fulfillment of these duties can be viewed as a set of performances, performance contracting would shift the manner in which these performances are evaluated for purposes of holding teachers and schools accountable for student learning:

> A performance contract is a legal agreement between a local school board and a supplier of instructional programs providing that the amount and schedule of payment will depend not on what services are said to have been provided, but on the degree of increase in student accomplishment, as independently audited in the field of the program.[1]

In other words, adequacy of performance on the part of the contracting agent, whether a teacher, school, or business firm, is not judged on the basis of what has been done or in relation to the effort made, but instead is judged in terms of student performance and rewarded accordingly.

Initial applications of this concept have taken the form of contracts between school systems and private firms, where the latter agree to achieve a predetermined level of performance with selected groups of children for a designated sum. If the firm is able to exceed expected results or to provide them within a time period shorter than that originally understood, bonuses may be given, but if they fail to satisfy the agreement, full or partial payment may be withheld. It is important to note that here student performance implies how well a student performs in relation to testing instruments, the presumption being that performance on a test or series of tests is indicative of both the student's achievement in relation to previously selected objectives and how adequately the contracting agent has performed in fulfilling contractual responsibilities. From a practical standpoint, then, measurement and testing are crucial factors in performance contracting arrangements. This type of relationship is illustrated by the contract drawn between the Texarkana School District and Dorsett Educational Systems,[2] in which it was agreed that Dorsett would be paid a certain amount for each child in grades six to eight whose performance in English and mathematics was raised by at least one grade level. The city of Gary, Indiana, entered a similar agreement with Behavior Research Laboratories, but with the difference that BRL was to assume responsibility for an entire school and its curriculum, while being paid for advances in math and reading as indicated by student achievement scores.[3]

The problem of indeterminate ends

Advocates of performance contracting argue that it is possible to formulate and measure specific performance objectives in business and that much the same can be done in education. But this position rests on the belief that educational ends and the means to their achievement are sufficiently analogous with those of business to use similar accountability procedures, an assumption open to question for several reasons. The first issue involves the *kinds* of results that are of primary interest to each of these fields. Most businesses are concerned with results involving products or services which are highly determinate in terms of their suitability for measurement, control, and standardization; all of which favor their accurate comparison with an ideal prototype and offer the advantage of high predictability. The crucial factor in all of this is their determinate quality. The limited extent to which this characteristic applies to a number of educational results is effectively argued by Pincoffs, whose interpretation of performance contracting is similar to ours; namely, that it generally refers to a practice in which teacher performance is evaluated in terms of student performance and rewarded accordingly. The argument he presents is worth following, for it represents a serious challenge to the assumption that most, if not all, educational outcomes can be translated into behavioral terms, observed and measured for purposes of accountability.

> We start with Frankena and others by saying that the proximate if not ultimate goal of education is the cultivation of excellences and that excellences are to be understood as desirable dispositions which are, in turn, informally defined as including abilities, habits, skills and traits of character or personality.[4]

A critical requirement of a performance contracting arrangement is that these excellences be defined in rather specific behavioral language so that student achievement can be accurately measured and teacher performance readily determined.

> To say that an excellence can be defined in behavioral terms is to say at least (1) that a sufficient condition of the presence of the excellence is that the pupil will, in specifiable circumstances behave in certain ways; (2) that the behavior is observable by persons other than the pupil himself; (3) that the behavior can in some way be measured.[5]

Pincoffs takes the position that if there are important excellences in education which cannot be defined in behavioral terms according to the preceding conditions, it follows they cannot be proper subjects for this form of educational accounting, and performance contracting would either be unacceptable as an educational practice or limited in its application to the extent that such excellences exist. According to Pincoffs, most excellences cannot be so defined because they are of an indeterminate nature:

> A determinate disposition is a disposition to act or react in the same or in similar ways whenever certain sorts of circumstances are present. For example, most people have a disposition to turn their heads when their name is

called behind their back, to sleep on their side, and to smile when someone smiles at them.[6]

But an intermediate disposition does not have this recurrent quality in particular kinds of situations, nor is it limited in the types of situations in which it might be displayed.

> An intermediate disposition, on the other hand, is a disposition which does not consist in my acting or reacting in the same or similar ways when certain sorts of circumstances are present. Wittiness, modesty, prudence, and love of animals will serve as examples. The witty person can exhibit his wit in a great variety of ways—by what he says on a great many very different sorts of occasions, by the cartoons that he draws, or by the impromptu verse that he composes. The modest person will hesitate to take credit for the deeds for which he is likely to be praised; he will avoid public or private eulogies; he will not want a monument or a monumental house or office, and so on.[7]

Therefore, a major feature of the intermediate disposition is that there is no way in which it can be adequately defined, that is, translated into behavioral terms or comprehensively encompassed from a performance standpoint.

> The 'and so on' is the mark of the indeterminate disposition. There is in principle no way to bring the list to an end as can be seen if we try to answer a child's question about what it is a man must do to be modest, or witty, or prudent, or to be a lover of animals. We can give him examples of what such a man would do; but if he wants to know if that is *all* that he must do, we will have to answer that it is not, that there is no 'all', that he has the wrong idea about the kind of thing modesty is . . . The modest person need not always stand behind another person, or run when he sees a reporter. There is no single sort of action or reaction which is in this way a necessary condition of his being modest; and in this way too, having an indeterminate disposition can be set off from having a determinate one.[8]

Consequently, a second characteristic is the absence of a necessary connection between having the disposition and acting or reacting in any particular way under a given set of circumstances whether contrived, as would be the case for purposes of testing, or otherwise. Pincoffs acknowledges that the development of determinate dispositions is necessary in education, and he offers the ability to spell accurately as an example of a disposition definable in behavioral terms, one which can be tested and in relation to which teachers presumably might be rewarded for developing. But the primary value of this disposition and so many others having a determinate quality is their contribution to higher order excellences which are more indeterminate in nature.

Let us take it for the sake of argument, for the time being, that spelling well is a necessary condition of making oneself understood by means of written language, that a bad speller is simply harder to understand. But writing in such a way as to be understood is, to the extent that writing is necessary for comprehension, a necessary condition of being able to explain or argue intelligibly. Being able to argue or explain intelligibly is a necessary condition of being articulate. But being able to argue or explain and being articulate are indeterminate excellences. They can be exhibited in a variety of ways, and there is no sense in asking what all the things are which a person must do to properly be called a competent explainer, arguer, or articulate.[9]

In other words, the indeterminate disposition cannot be defined in behavioral terms for the reason that "it cannot be analyzed into a *sum* of determinate dispositions, just as we cannot give a child a finite list of (relatively) determinate things a person must do to be prudent, wise, careful, judicious, imaginative, considerate, efficient, clear-headed or humane."[10] While Pincoffs does not attempt to defend a particular set of educational excellences, one may conclude from his argument that if many results appropriate to education do consist in excellences of this nature, then they cannot be defined in behavioral terms either, and educational accountability in the form of performance contracting would be impracticable where they are concerned.

The concept of an educated person

As we shall see, several writers believe these excellences do exist and must be viewed as important aims in education. But beyond Pincoff's examples, what kinds of things are we talking about? Two avenues of discussion will be pursued to arrive at a better understanding of these dispositions and the importance of their development as aims in education.

The first approach focuses on the everyday world in which we live and asks: What skills and abilities will be necessary to ensure our future survival, our economic viability as a nation in competition with other nations of the world, and what human qualities will be necessary for the maintenance and improvement of our culture and for the individual to find a meaningful place within it? Our technical and social milieu continues to generate problems of staggering complexity, and is doing so at an ever increasing rate. A situation complicated by the fact that due to our greater interdependence changes in one dimension of life often are attended by implications nonlinear in their effect. A prolonged and critical shortage of energy would not simply mean that people have to forego the comfort of air conditioning or the pleasure of a Sunday drive, but loss of jobs, relocation of families, severely altered lifestyles, as well as national and international crises. The greenhouse effect that is now developing in our atmosphere poses serious implications for future climactic conditions and food production, and may force the massive relocation of coastal communities due to dramatic increases in sea level. The sharp birthrate decline between 1961 and 1977 was cumulative and most pronounced after 1971. One of the more immediate effects of this decline was on elementary school enrollments, but ultimately it meant that colleges and universities had to come to terms with a rapidly changing eighteen-year-old population, sharply diminished in numbers and altered in its racial and ethnic composition, a problem that will be even more pronounced between the years 1989 and 1995. Institutions of higher education will not be the only group experiencing intense competition for a dramatically changing constituent market; other consumer markets certainly will be impacted as the average age of the population increases, with attendant demands for different forms of health care, living arrangements and consumer products. Unless addressed, these changes could pose a serious threat to our future productivity as a nation, and do so at a time when we are experiencing stronger competition from other economies of the world.

Analysis of the changes experienced by this nation and others throughout the post World War II period prompted writers such as Postman and Weingartner to observe that the very nature of change itself is changing, and being able to deal with it effectively presents one of the most difficult challenges to our survival.[11] The challenge to which these authors referred was basically twofold, and is equally relevant today. On the one hand, there is the need to monitor change and its ramifications as they are played out in various facets of our economic and social life, the need to understand what is presently happening and to anticipate its probable consequences. But though change and "megatrends" appear to be an inevitable feature of life, their direction does not always have to be set in a predetermined and unalterable pattern. Scientists are justified in their concern about the future and spend considerable time gathering data for the purpose of predicting it, for the purpose of answering the question "What will life be like ten, twenty or one hundred years from now?" But attention also must be given to the normative question "What *should* life be like?" Are there ways of living and perspectives on life that are preferable to those now within our experience and, if so, how might they be brought into being? Are there changes that ought to be initiated now to avoid future consequences that may be undesirable and yet seem inevitable if the changes necessary for their avoidance are not undertaken now? The philosophical questions—How ought we to treat one another? In what does the good life consist, and how might such a life be achieved and maintained? predate Socrates, but they remain with us today. To know where we are heading as a people is extremely important, but it becomes far more meaningful if we have some idea of where we should be going.

Providing a humane standard of living within an acceptable level of inflation, meeting energy needs while maintaining environmental quality, striving to assure greater efficiency and integrity in government, our professions, and business, and developing worthwhile goals for the future are among our most pressing challenges. Solving the technical problems they pose will involve factual and empirical considerations, but coming to terms with these issues will require that we also establish priorities and make difficult choices from among alternative needs and conflicting interests. They will require us to make normative judgments about our values, responsibilities, and obligations. Surely, a question that should be of paramount concern to educators and others responsible for the development of children is- What knowledge, skills, and personal qualities must our children have if they are to address these problems and make the difficult decisions and choices that will be required?

Postman and Weingartner speak of entropy, "a general and unmistakable tendency of all systems—natural and man-made—in the universe to 'run down,' to reduce to chaos and uselessness." They argue that schools should further individual powers of critical thought and inquiry by which attitudes, beliefs, and assumptions that foster this condition can be subverted, and the processes of entropy restrained.[12]

After visiting several hundred schools across the country and surveying the contemporary scene during this same period, Silberman reached the conclusion that "what tomorrow needs is not masses of intellectuals, but masses of educated men—men educated to feel and to act as well as to think." In support of this he points to the experience of the German university under Hitler, and the fact that the crematoria were often presided over by men who enjoyed Wagner and Mozart.

> What we must also realize—what I should have known from my own upbringing, and what three and a half years of sitting in on public school and college classes and immersing myself in the mass media drove home to me—is that education is inescapably a moral as well as intellectual and aesthetic enterprise.[13]

History and the German experience provide ample evidence that the narrow intellectualism characteristic of the Nazi movement was neither synonymous with the concept of being reasonable, nor with the disposition to be reflective and critical in one's moral and social life. Without such dispositions it is doubtful whether this or any society could possess the moral autonomy necessary to resist a regime which demands total and unquestioned obedience to its authority. It is not Silberman's position that we need people who are any less knowledgeable, but rather that more than ever our society requires individuals who are willing to act on principle; people who are morally and intellectually concerned and recognize the importance of this concern in meeting the problems we face.

Our second approach to these questions is more philosophical, but directly related. If these human qualities are required to meet the foregoing challenges, then from a practical standpoint it is clear that their development must be of primary concern to educators, let alone those who occupy positions of leadership and are responsible for planning the future. In fact, the various dispositions and qualities identified by these writers have a direct bearing on what it means to live a rational and democratic life. By such a life we imply a society where primary institutions are essentially structured on democratic principles and ideally where procedures in human affairs are guided by reasoning and all that is implied by the notion of being reasonable. The argument we wish to advance will be criticized for being too idealistic, a criticism we shall address later. But for the present it must be explained, because the argument has a direct bearing on the aims we should pursue in education and on the implications that various interpretations of accountability can have for students and their teachers. Quite simply, our position shall be that it is a major responsibility of the school to develop an appreciation for human rights, to promote an understanding of democratic principles and rational behavior, and to provide experiences that have the effect of furthering such understanding.

A rational life, after all, is fundamentally different from a life nonrationally oriented, where decisions of consequence are customarily reached on the basis of whim, superstition, or arbitrary degree. Here we follow Peters's argument that any individual or people who seek to know the reason why of things must become committed to a pursuit that is identifiably rational in procedure and in many situations public in form; assuming, of course, that they are serious in wanting to discover truthful, accurate or meaningful answers to their concerns, are open to serious consideration of the answers which objective inquiry reveals, and are at least mindful of the limitations on their understanding which prejudice and uninformed preconceptions can impose.[14]

Whether the question is "What ought I to do?" in regard to some personal matter, "What is the best policy for my company?" or "How can I most effectively help this student?" a situation is implied in which those concerned must somehow *discover* and *choose* what is preferable or right from among alternative and sometimes conflicting possibilities.[15] A course of action or proposed state of affairs is alternative to others by virtue of having distinctive features which set it apart and in the end often become significant reasons for its selection or avoidance. In making choices we expect people to have reasons for what they say and do and on appropriate occasions to reveal their reasons as an element in justifying a particular decision or course they have chosen. Our scientist in the first chapter clearly illustrates this point. He may establish and test certain scientific hypotheses and on the basis of his findings reach a number of conclusions. If he publishes his conclusions or is asked to present them at a scientific conference, he will be expected to have reasons to support them and, if requested, to reveal his reasons for scrutiny by his colleagues. Though they may acknowledge that research in his area is very difficult and understand that his conclusions are only tentative, pending further study, this would not change their expectation that he have reasons for presenting his present position and be able to offer them as a justification for it. True, his colleagues may disagree with the reasons he presents, believe that they are shallow or foolish, but the crucial element in all of this is that we expect to have reasons given. A rational life presupposes questioning, analysis, reasoning, and ultimately having reasons to support the beliefs and opinions we hold, the decisions we make and the courses of action we choose to follow. If such a life is to have meaning and endure, then the procedures by which these reasons are sought, arrived at, presented and ultimately reviewed must be taken seriously by those who subscribe to it.

Where problems of an ethical or moral nature are concerned, the characteristics of a rational life require much of a person, implying a need for deliberation, autonomy, and recognition of personal values and principles which often must be measured against standards that are public and somewhat independent from the individual.

A man who is faced with such a [moral] problem knows that it is his own problem, and that nobody can answer it for him. He may, it is true, ask the advice of other people; and he may also ascertain more facts about the circumstances and consequences of a proposed action, and other facts of this sort. But there will come a time when he does not hope to find out anything else of relevance by factual inquiry, and when he knows that, whatever others may say about the answer to his problem, he has to answer it . . . For one of the most important constituents of our freedom, as moral agents, is the freedom to form our own opinions about moral questions . . .[16]

But this sense of freedom is not to be confused with another.

Against this conviction, which every adult has, that he is free to form his own opinions about moral questions, we have to set another characteristic of these questions which seems to contradict it. That is, that the answering of moral questions is or ought to be a rational activity. Although most of us think that we are free to form our own opinion about moral questions, we do not feel that it does not matter what we think about them—that the answering of moral questions is a quite arbitrary business, like the choice of one postage stamp from the sheet rather than another. We feel, rather, that it matters very much what answer we give, and that the finding of an answer is a task that should engage our rational powers to the limit of their capacity. So the freedom that we have in morals is to be distinguished from the freedom which comes when it simply does not matter what we do or say.[17]

It may be arguable whether people generally employ their rational powers to the degree suggested, but where decisions and actions significantly affect the lives of others or one's own we assume that they should. Thus, the freedom to choose morally is a freedom carefully exercised in the life presented. However, one's freedom in such matters is further circumscribed by the fact that morality is

> a social enterprise, not just a discovery or invention of the individual for his own guidance. Like one's language, state, or church, it exists before the individual, who is inducted into it, and it goes on existing after him . . . Morality . . . is also social in its origins, sanctions, and functions. It is an instrument of society as a whole for the guidance of individuals and smaller groups. It makes demands on individuals which are, initially at least, external to them . . . If they come to disagree with the demands, then, as Socrates thought and as we shall see later, they must still do so from the moral point of view which has somehow been inculcated into them.[18]

This dimension is difficult to deny not only in morality but in other areas of social concern. Having reasons is indeed important, but this does not mean that all would be relevant, valid or acceptable. There also must exist certain standards and forms of appraisal by which reasons and the decisions they support can be assessed. Neither the standards nor these forms are entirely private. Groups within society have conventions, attitudes, values and beliefs which comprise the essence of such standards and guide their appraisals, and according to which various acts and reasons are deemed appropriate or inappropriate, justifying or irrelevant. Public standards and values suggest to the members of a society that in some spheres of conduct and opinion, what they do is of concern to society and would tend to condition their freedom in such matters to the extent that this larger concern presses for conformity.

At the same time, in a rational life, public values and procedures are not without condition, nor is the foregoing antinomy between freedom and reason overdrawn. For if a society adopts or pursues a life in which reasoning and justification are said to count, such activities would surely lack point if its members were *normally* unfree to do what they have found good reasons for doing. As Peters so effectively argued, within a rational society a presumption exists in favor of having the freedom to do what is supported by reason unless there are relevant considerations to justify its restriction.[19] In essence, this type of life not only requires that those adopting it be free to think and to act, but that just cause be shown for any infringement on their freedom to do so by those who would impose it.

For this reason, political and social arrangements would be equally important and of concern to any person who truly values the advantages such a life has to offer and understands how precarious its underpinnings can be. Political institutions, especially, would have to be designed to protect the freedoms of thought and action this form of life requires, incorporating procedures by which the need for constraint and its proper form can be determined and justly applied. Furthermore, what sense would it make for a people to aspire to a rational way of living if only to be subject to the authority of institutions which by design are contrary to its purposes? It seems essential, then, that governmental institutions embody to the maximum extent possible the very features they have been established to protect. We expect governments to have reasons when they go to war, make laws or restrict freedom because these matters are of great importance to those affected; but if a rational existence is to have any meaning, the reasons which underlie the actions of government must be made known, for to do so acknowledges the "reasonableness" of a people and their right to critically judge what is of greatest significance in their lives.[20] Where governments are structurally open to critical appraisal by those whom they govern and purportedly serve, it is a matter of logic that simply having reasons is not enough; if the appraisal is to occur and be informed, reasons must be revealed for examination. It is presumed, then, that in addition to there being reasons for things, occasionally these reasons must be revealed, exchanged and evaluated.

At the same time, it is quite possible to acknowledge a general necessity for having reasons without being committed to the notion that it is always appropriate to reveal them, or that a demand for their publicity would always be desirable or just. We also expect governments to act on matters, such as military or international, without always publicizing their nature, and while we may have reasons for much of what we do in our work and personal lives, we reject the notion that everyone is entitled to know what they are. The most that can be said for the present is that if individuals or a people choose this form of existence, they must satisfy its basic presuppositions. The latter would include, among other considerations, the presumption favoring freedom of thought, action and choice; having reasons for what is done; and presenting these reasons for the critical review of others when doing so is appropriate and justified.

We assume that a rational life finds its most complete expression in societies where people value its unique contributions and where the freedom to question and inquire, to openly express and exchange ideas, and to individually participate in the transactions of reasoning are protected by institutional arrangements.

Where societies aspire to this form of existence and structure their institutions accordingly, major responsibilities are imposed on their members if they are to survive. The implications for the education of youth are of paramount importance in terms of the skills and dispositions they must acquire. Scheffler identifies several dispositions which characterize a rational approach to life and notes what is required in the process of their development.

> To cultivate this trait is to liberate the mind from dogmatic adherence to prevalent ideological fashions, as well as the dictates of authority. For the rational mind is encouraged to go behind such fashions and dictates and to ask for their justification, whether the issue be factual or practical. In training our students to reason we train them to be critical. We encourage them to ask questions, to look for evidence, to seek and scrutinize alternatives, to be critical of their own ideas as well as those of others. This educational course precludes taking schooling as an instrument for shaping their minds to a preconceived idea. For if they seek reasons, it is their evaluation of such reasons that will determine what ideas they eventually accept.[21]

Other skills and dispositions are implied as well, since the various forms of accounting discussed earlier must play a role. It is largely by means of describing, relating, reporting, offering explanations and justifying analyses that we convey our reasons for what we believe and do and submit them for the critical evaluation of others. In expecting our scientist to offer reasons in support of his hypotheses we are really expecting him to give an account of his work and to a certain extent of himself. And when our government decides to invade a country, change our tax structure or implement policies which affect our lives, we expect the president and others who are responsible to account for their actions by explaining and presenting their reasons as a form of justification. The forms of accounting discussed in chapter 1 are indispensable to communication: Without them rational behavior could not occur in the sense we have been describing. Consequently, developing the skills required by these forms of accounting must be included among the aims of education; in other words, schools must assist students to become progressively more effective at accounting for themselves and for those matters and responsibilities in relation to which they may be held accountable in their student and adult life.

Although our list of educational outcomes may not be complete, we include among them the skills in communication these forms of accounting presuppose, the ability to question, to think critically, to analyze and propose solutions to problems, as well as the disposition to be reasonable, for ostensibly all are implied by what it means to be rational and are essential to institutions democratic in structure. Moreover, in light of our modern day experience, a case can be made that our future survival may very well depend on the development of these dispositions, yet many are relatively indeterminate in terms of the behavioral requirements identified by Pincoffs, and certainly all are far more indeterminate than most "results" of concern to modern business.

Two arguments have been advanced to arrive at the position that these excellences should be viewed as major aims in education. The first focused on the problems and issues confronting us as a society; the second was more philosophical, emphasizing the basic features of a rational and democratic form of existence and what such an existence would require of institutions and those who participate in it. The latter argument may be criticized for being too idealistic and out of touch with reality, but this criticism only has value in reminding us that human beings and the institutions they design often fall short of the goals their ideals represent; it does not mean that ideals can be discarded, nor invalidate the role they must play in everyday life. The basic principles embodied within the Declaration of Independence, our Constitution and the Bill of Rights give central importance to the ideals of freedom, equal consideration and justice, the dignity of the individual and the notion that individuals should not be arbitrarily excluded from life's opportunities. History and our everyday practices as a people indicate that we often have not lived up to these ideals, but this does not mean that they should be abandoned.

The tensions that developed throughout the sixties and seventies over the issue of civil rights for women and minorities reflected a greater awareness of the disparity that had developed between what we espouse as fundamental beliefs for our society and what we actually were doing as a people. The civil rights movement represents a continuing struggle to diminish this disparity by attempting to bring the actions and social practices of this nation more into line with its ideals. Since the principles upon which it was founded embody these ideals and actually define what our national character ought to be, infidelity to such principles over a prolonged period of time would not only threaten the present and intended character of this nation, but clearly bring into question whether we really are what we say we are as a people, and whether we really believe in what we espouse as ideals. In this respect, by promoting greater fidelity to these principles the efforts and achievements made on behalf of human rights during this century have served not only the particular groups involved but also the interests of the nation as a whole.

We operate on a similar assumption when we establish aims in education. The goals and objectives we set for the education of our youth are really a statement of the things we believe are important both for this society and for their development. Yet in establishing these broader aims we realize that ultimately every child will not become knowledgeable, be a good writer, be skilled in communication or adept at critical thinking; nevertheless, these ideals must exist as aims to guide the education of our youth, much as ideals must exist to guide the institutions and practices of society.

Basic skills and the issue of educational priorities

Some accountability proponents would concede Pincoffs's argument and probably acknowledge the abilities and dispositions we have noted, but nevertheless expect performance contracting to be employed as the primary means for ensuring greater accountability in education.

> True education also has objectives that are difficult to measure or even define clearly, such as 'maturity' or 'high motivation'. But the fact that education is greater than the sum of its measurable parts should not deter us from obtaining reliable data on those parts that do lend themselves to definition and measurement. In concentrating on these parts, such as the basic skills, we must of course make sure that our instruments and judgments accurately assess the range of things that are important to know, not only what is easiest to measure.[22]

On the surface this appears to be a sound argument. Pincoffs's point concerning the nature of determinate dispositions and their role in providing a foundation for more indeterminate excellences highlights the function and relative importance of basic skills in education. By skills we usually imply abilities of a particular sort. Most people have the ability to swing and stretch their arms; daily they perform a myriad of unconscious movements involving eye-hand coordination, but few have these abilities developed to the level of proficiency necessary for fielding or batting in the major baseball leagues, certainly not with the skill for a .300 average. Being a skilled baseball player requires several concomitant abilities such as a sense of timing, coordination and selective responses to different styles of pitching and game strategy, most of which are by no means innate but must be acquired through long periods of study and practice. We say that one player possesses more skill than another when he has perfected these abilities to a more advanced degree, his mastery being evidenced in performances which are more consistent, dependable and on the whole much better.

A skill, then, is an acquired competence; the ability to perform and function purposefully in particular ways under given sets of conditions. For this reason, skills can be viewed as vesting certain residual powers in those who possess them, a potential for future performance which can be summoned or actualized whenever the circumstances of life demand. To say that a skill is *basic* simply means that it is fundamental to something else, a necessary condition of some further outcome. In baseball a sense of timing and coordination are basic to hitting a ball; and, of course, hitting a ball is a skill basic to earning runs, winning the game and so forth.

Much of what has been said about skills in baseball can be said of those associated with learning. Auditory and visual discrimination, proper eye movement, a sense of space and configuration are basic to word recognition and the higher skills of reading. Interestingly, these abilities and a number of more complex skills such as reading, speech, or computation, derive value from their utility; that is, because the skill in question is necessary or instrumental to some further activity, goal or level of achievement. Reading skills become valuable when one is asked to complete a job application, or when one is seeking the knowledge, information or enjoyment contained in books and other printed material. For the most part skills associated with the elementary and middle school years have these features. Some are simply more basic than others and should be viewed as occupying a particular place in a developmental hierarchy that eventually leads to the acquisition of skills which are far more intricate and complex in terms of the cognition and performances they require. If it is true that basic skills such as being able to read, write, spell, and compute are relatively more determinate and respectively essential to being articulate, becoming a competent engineer or understanding the problems just mentioned, why not use performance contracting to hold teachers accountable at least where they are concerned?

Few would argue the point that the abilities to communicate, read and compute are important in the life of an individual, for on these skills hinge opportunities for a life more enriching. In spite of the electronic revolution, the many advances that have occurred in the media through which we are informed and have access to daily events, reading continues to offer a major channel for enjoyment and personal advancement. The absence of these skills imposes a serious limitation on any individual living within a complex society; consequently, their emphasis should receive high priority in this nation's schools especially during the early and middle years of schooling. But even during these years assigning a high priority to the development of basic skills does not require that they be given exclusive attention. In determining educational priorities we must distinguish those which are logically prior from those which are of longer-term concern. Without question, by their nature basic skills are more determinate and because of this more easily measured, but they are basic because they represent a foundation for the higher-order excellences we have identified. However important and prerequisite these skills may be, it is equally apparent that more will be required of our students if they are to meet the various challenges noted above. It is one thing to be able to read and quite another to have the disposition to use this skill throughout one's life to further knowledge and to acquire the understanding which intelligent citizenship increasingly demands. Acquiring basic skills and being vocationally competent are of central importance to be sure, but as Peters has noted, we expect more from an educated person than having a knack, skill, or for that matter simply knowing something.

A man might be a very highly trained scientist; yet we might refuse to call him an educated man. This would not be because there is nothing worth-while about science; for it is a supreme example of a worth-while activity. It would not be because such a man cares nothing about it and has no grasp of its principles; for the hypothesis is that he is dedicated to it and has got a good grounding of principles. What then is lacking which might make us withhold the description of being 'educated' from such a man? It is surely a lack of what might be called 'cognitive perspective.' The man could have a very limited conception of what he is doing. He could work away at science without seeing its connection with much else, its place in a coherent pattern of life. For him it is an activity cognitively adrift.[23]

Peters is correct in stressing the distinction between merely being trained and having this perspective. Consistent with our earlier discussion, it is essential to the welfare of all that scientists question what they do and how it might affect others, to have a perspective on how they and their work relate to other aspects of life. But scientists are not alone in this; it is becoming more and more evident that whether a person happens to hold high political office or happens to be a plumber, production worker, lawyer, doctor or teacher, what they do affects others and determines the quality of others' lives as well as their own.

The cognitive perspective to which Peters refers closely parallels what it means to be a rational person and requires that the individual possess a number of abilities in relation to which performance contracting would be impracticable as a form of accountability. We assume that educated men and women will be competent in basic skills and that they will be knowledgeable, but we also expect them to possess this broader perspective evidenced in their disposition to question and to seek an understanding of the "why" of things; in other words, to reflect in their behavior the very excellences we have been discussing. True, certain dispositions such as being rational, morally concerned, having a sense of justice and responsibility cannot be appraised in a single or limited number of instances, but they are revealed as individual qualities over an extended period of time. The parent who is concerned that his children develop a sense of responsibility certainly operates on this assumption. Innumerable situations may arise in which, by discussion, admonition, the assigning of responsibilities or holding a child answerable for his actions, a parent hopes to contribute to the development of this disposition and the attitudes upon which it depends. Yet a single or limited number of instances in which a child may behave responsibly or irresponsibly cannot be taken as being clearly definitive of his character; it can only be said that he has acted responsibly or irresponsibly on those occasions. To determine the former would require a much longer period of observation of many different kinds of situations such that on balance we would be justified in saying that in our opinion this person tends to be responsible or irresponsible. However subjective such judgments appear to be, they are frequently made, and they are made about a great many dispositions which have this indeterminate quality but which, nevertheless, we consider to be important and believe can be positively or negatively influenced.

Those who share responsibility for the education of children have the difficult task of deciding which outcomes to pursue while children are in school and selecting methods that are appropriate for bringing them about. The fact that basic skills are fundamental and therefore of critical importance to the development of children is not the issue. The issue is whether a system of accountability which rewards or punishes for only a very restricted range of outcomes will encourage or even allow the kind of attention more indeterminate excellences require. What is to be expected from a group of educators who operate under a system which offers incentives only for results that are quantifiable as a measure of successful teaching? Lessinger appears sensitive to this problem when he states that in concentrating on the basic skills care must be taken that "our instruments and judgments accurately assess the range of things important to know, not only what is easiest to measure."[24] Yet other statements seem to belie this concern.

> Once we have standardized reliable data on the cost of producing a variety of educational results using a variety of methods, our legislators and school officials will at last be able to draw up budgets based on facts instead of vague assertions. Through the knowledge gained in this process of management, we will also be able to hold the schools accountable for results.[25]

But will these budgets then allocate for programs designed to further outcomes which are not as readily measured on a cost/benefit basis; for example, a program concerned with furthering values and their clarification? What about art, music, discussion seminars which center on contemporary problems, and the like? The BRL group had contracted to assume responsibility for an entire school program, which means a comprehensive curriculum, yet investigation by the Indiana Department of Public Instruction revealed that subjects other than the ones for which BRL was to be paid and held accountable were being neglected.[26] At issue are educational priorities and the relative importance that would be assigned to various outcomes under this form of accountability. Faced with an array of statistical data on student achievement in basic skills, will the school board member expect similar data from all areas of the school program? And, if it is not forthcoming, will he or she make the questionable assumption that because certain outcomes are not suscepti- ble to precise measurement, there is little point in allocating money for them, or that they are of dubious benefit?

Advocates of performance contracting could argue that over the years points of view have varied considerably about which educational aims to pursue in teaching children, often depending on prevailing philoso- phies of education and which theory was most in vogue at the time. We have had traditional education with emphasis on discipline, the three R's and other basic skills, progressive education with more attention to the social sciences and student interaction, the open classroom with an emphasis on self-directed learning and so forth. And so, why blame performance contracting for changing currents in educational thought?

This argument has a measure of truth; even in the absence of performance contracting arrangements, schools and other agencies concerned about the welfare of children can have a very narrow interpretation of their mission. Decisions about learning objectives and what will or will not be emphasized in the classroom often depend on the consensual values of the community, whatever philosophies of education predominate, as well as the availability and commitment of resources a community is willing to make. We noted the Sputnik era when large sums of money were provided by the federal government for programs in math and science in an effort to "close the gap" that had allegedly developed between American youth and children in the Soviet Union. And under tax reform measures, scarcer revenues have affected curricula in many school systems. But acknowledgment of the preceding does not obviate the concern we have raised. Too many proposals for performance contracting incorporate a reward system suitable only for a very restricted range of measurable outcomes. In this respect, unless it is applied with caution and with a broader view of education in mind, it will only exacerbate the problem of school curricula which, in some communities, already are too narrowly defined and extremely circumscribed from the standpoint of student needs and the future needs of this country.

Student values and the hidden curriculum

There is the additional problem of the strategies employed by contractors to assure the results for which they will be paid and the potential influence of these methods on teacher and student attitudes, the climate of the school, and ultimately on educational outcomes. Hottleman has noted a number of practices that have occurred during the course of several performance contracts, two of which follow:

> Item: In Hartford, Conn., where Alpha Systems, Inc., holds the contract, a serious proposal (rejected by teachers) was made that pinball machines and slot machine pool tables be installed in the schools. Children would be permitted access to these recreational outlets as a reward for learning, with a portion of the money in the till to go to the school system and a portion to the performance contractor. Item: In the Bronx, where Learning Foundations . . . holds the contract, children were pre-tested in one large group in an assembly hall at 95 degrees temperature for five hours in one day. Learning Foundations' rate of payment depends upon the difference between initial pre-test scores and later scores computed from tests conducted under much

more favorable circumstances. Also, the Bronx project incorporates a reward system of green stamps for learning (a common practice among performance contractors). Children are given a cheaply-printed company catalogue displaying toy guns and other merchandise which is used to motivate achievement.[27]

Positive reinforcement can take many forms and admittedly is important to most of us, but how would it be interpreted under these procedures?

> The Bronx project is typical. If a student learns at a predetermined accelerated rate . . . he may earn enough green stamps to get a toy gun. 'Why do you learn Johnny?' 'To get a gun, of course.' When measurement becomes king and profit the motive, reading, for example, does not become 'reading for pleasure' or 'reading for appreciation' or reading for 'leisure or understanding', but straight de-coding or 'reading for profit.'[28]

It might be rejoined that other forms of reinforcement could be used which are much less material, such as praise or a "pat on the back," but how would a perceptive youngster view such gestures under contracting arrangements? Would the student tend to believe the teacher is offering encouragement because he genuinely hopes the student will succeed in skills that are in the student's best interest, or would these gestures be interpreted to mean: "You obviously want me to try harder so my test scores will be higher and your profits greater." A major criticism growing out of the Texarkana contract was "evidence of teaching for the test" in order to improve post-test results.

The points we are raising must be given thoughtful consideration by any person who takes the moral implications of teaching seriously. There is a mystique about technology and industry which evolves around the belief that if it is possible for technology to put astronauts on the moon, the procedures which have contributed to this achievement can make whatever seems possible a reality, whether it is solving a technical problem, providing a remedy for major social ills or educating children. Although the recent space shuttle disaster brought home the reality that technology and human judgment are not infallible, the unfortunate result of this mystique is its tendency to promote a mechanistic view of children and their learning.

> Modern curriculum theory, currently being influenced by systems analysis, tends to regard the child simply as input inserted into one end of a great machine, from which he eventually emerges at the other end as output replete with all the behaviors, the 'competencies,' and the skills for which he has been programmed . . . Even when the output is differentiated, such a mechanistic conception of education contributes only to man's regimentation and dehumanization, rather than to his autonomy.[29]

Supporters of performance contracting seem to assume that the only results occurring at the end of an educational process are those which have been planned; that learning is little more than a matter of so many inputs to produce a certain kind and number of outputs. This ignores much that has been revealed through educational research regarding moral development, incidental learning, and what has been termed the "hidden curriculum." The experiential world of children must be viewed as a totality which includes innumerable experiences that convey as much if not more to them about life than what we explicitly state or contrive for their learning. After several years of study on the moral development of children and adults, Kohlberg and his colleagues have found that values and moral perceptions are influenced as much by what we do as by what we say; by the kinds of values and attitudes which we ourselves truly hold and reveal to children through the choices we make, by the way in which we go about our work and the manner in which we relate to others. Actions do speak louder than words.

> If you want to develop morality or a sense of justice in kids, you have to create a just school, a just classroom environment. For the fact is that much of what kids learn comes not from books and materials, but from the moral environment and atmosphere that you establish in your classroom—your hidden curriculum.[30]

The same point applies to the home environment. A child is more likely to be influenced by knowledge of his father's infidelity or by the fact that he may be cheating in his business than he is likely to be by regular lectures on honesty. If some programs have been willing to pre-test under extraordinary and unfair conditions or to cheat by teaching for the test, to what lengths might others go if either their profits, tenure, salary, promotion, budget or merit are based on how well their students perform under a performance contracting arrangement? And what will be the long-term effect on the children they are teaching? Consequently, educators must be just as concerned about the climate they establish within a school and the methods they employ to achieve educational aims as they are about which outcomes to pursue.

Because of the foregoing, a more comprehensive concept of accountability is necessary for education, but developing such a concept commits us to a problem of some proportion. It would be unfair and unproductive simply to criticize perceived weaknesses in performance contracting without offering some insight into the problems identified. For example, several forms of accounting were presented as the first element of accountability, and we have argued that these forms of accounting are indispensable to communication and a rational life because it is by means of reporting, describing, explaining and offering justifying analyses that we reveal our reasons for things and communicate them to others.

Because of their role in communication and the fact that our daily affairs often require that we account to others, we took the position that developing the skills necessary to adequately account for oneself must be included among the central aims of education, along with basic skills and other more indeterminate excellences. However, an interpretation of how these forms of accounting should specifically relate to the accountability of students and their teachers has yet to be discussed. Furthermore, in criticizing the use of rewards and other motivational incentives associated with performance contracting, we cannot ignore the fact that an extensive amount of research in the area of operant conditioning theory suggests that people need incentives and are motivated to greater achievement when they are positively reinforced in their efforts. Our criticism of the use of such strategies did not stem from a belief that personal rewards and incentives should not be used in education, but reflected a concern with several abuses that have occurred and will continue to occur unless such strategies are applied with common sense and a broader perspective concerning their role and relative value. In the following chapters we must attempt to provide this perspective if the position we are taking is to have any cogency.

Moreover, while various forms of accounting have been identified as a primary element in accountability, other elements are equally important and involve the concepts of responsibility, obligation and agent compliance, as well as several factors which affect the quality of accountability relationships. Issues relating to these elements also must be explored and their relevance to education demonstrated. For example, in taking the position that rational behavior requires that we have reasons for what we do and that the forms of accounting we have been discussing be the primary means by which we convey our reasons to others, we also realize that it is not always appropriate or required that we reveal them. Situations exist in which the issue of our doing so is largely a matter of personal choice. And yet, as we have noted, more is implied by the notion of being "obligated" or "subject to" giving an account than a situation in which the matter of its provision rests solely on the discretion of the accountant.

Why should teachers be accountable or have to answer for student performance? In this chapter several aims have been identified which we believe teachers and schools have a responsibility to promote. From the standpoint of student learning, should schools and teachers be accountable for *having* the responsibility to promote these aims, or should they be accountable for their ultimate fulfillment, as accountability proponents seem to demand? Do teachers and the school represent the most significant factors influencing student learning? To hold them accountable under typical performance-contracting arrangements implies that they are. And if this is so, what responsibilities do students and their parents have for learning and student performance? These questions are relevant to the debate over accountability in education, but before they can be addressed in any meaningful way we must examine the basis for accountability obligations. If being obligated to do something does represent some cost to an agent's freedom, then the conditions under which we can become accountable or answerable to others represent an additional element in this concept.

PART II

The obligation to account

CHAPTER 3

The basis for accountability relationships

Although the various forms of accounting described in chapter 1 are essential to communication, the circumstances under which such accounts are given often vary in regard to what is expected and the degree of personal discretion one may have in meeting such expectations. Offering an explanation about our business affairs to a friend in response to a casual question, where our doing so is simply a matter of personal consideration, seems fundamentally different from those occasions on which we feel we *should* or *must* explain them, occasions in which we realize that our freedom to refuse is more limited and circumscribed by considerations extending beyond our own. For example, we might tell our friend that we would rather not discuss the matter because it is too personal. Although he may be disappointed at not being taken into our confidence, in all likelihood he would recognize our right to privacy and acknowledge that even within the bounds of friendship it is our affair, not his, and there is no reason why we have to tell him. The same would not be true in a court of law, where we have a *legal obligation* to report on such matters; nor would it be true under all circumstances involving our friend. Suppose that a few months earlier he loaned us a large sum of money to invest in our business, and that he now wishes to know how the business is doing and requests an explanation concerning the status of the loan. If our initial agreement involved a formal contract, we might very well have a legal obligation to respond, but even in the absence of a formal contract, if we borrowed the money under the conditions of friendship and a promise to repay, there are grounds for saying that we have a *moral* or an *ethical obligation* to give an explanation. I think we would agree that our privilege of remaining silent has been conditioned by the fact that our friend has a personal stake in the matter, and that now he too has a claim or at least a moral entitlement that he did not have before.

In the present chapter we shall examine the basis for accountability obligations. Our discussion will focus on an analysis of two concepts—"responsibility" and "entitlement"—which I shall argue incorporate the minimum conditions necessary to validate the assignment of any accountability obligation and whatever interagent relationship it may entail. As prerequisites for establishing accountability obligations and relationships, both concepts provide at least prima facie grounds for accountability in education, the topic concluding this chapter.

Responsibility: the initial validating condition

We shall begin with the position that *responsibility* is a necessary though not a sufficient condition for the assignment of any obligation, including the obligation to account. Obligations are normally generated by the acts of individuals or groups in conjunction with those institutions and practices of a society that define such acts to be obligating.[1] Acknowledged, then, are the institutions of law, conventional morality, and various bodies of rules and principles by which people govern and regulate their affairs. Our initial position is that two factors underlie any obligation: (1) various social institutions and practices that play a role in identifying which acts are obligating; and (2) those *acts,* so defined, which constitute at least prima facie grounds for saying that an obligation exists.

The foregoing is illustrated in cases involving a promise by one party to another. Suppose that Smith borrows something from a friend. Though he may not state his intention of returning the item, his act carries the implication of a promise, for central to the idea of "borrowing" something is the condition that it be returned. Conventional morality, certain theories of ethics, and occasionally the formal requirements of law support the view that such an act does create an obligation and that Smith is obligated to do something in the future because his prior act has incurred the full range of performance normally associated with the concept of borrowing.

But it is important to note that while the act of borrowing is considered obligating, the obligation itself may be *attributed* to Smith only because he is in some sense responsible. Responsibility becomes a necessary consideration in relationships of this nature because the assignment of any obligation is usually contingent upon identifying the person or parties responsible for the act creating it. Now some may object that the element of responsibility is by no means essential for an obligation to exist. For example, if A were told by B that "something of value has been borrowed" and A remained uninformed concerning the responsible party's identity, he would likely recognize an obligation to return the item anyway, reaching this conclusion solely on the knowledge of what it means to borrow and that something in fact has been borrowed. There is a sense in which this argument is true but at the same time misses the point. The concept of obligation generally has practical application in relationships between two or more parties. If the obligation is substantive, it must be someone's or some agent's. The point to be emphasized is not so much that responsibility is prerequisite to the obligation, which it is, but that it is necessary for making it Smith's obligation. The formerly stated determinants, i.e., acts and defining institutions, do hold, but would have to be extended to include the element of responsibility where such an assignment is required. In the present example we must distinguish (1) an act, (2) the obligation which it brings into being as a result of the institutions mentioned, and (3) responsibility for the act in light of which the obligation may be justly attributed.

Though both are related, a rather sharp distinction has been drawn between what Smith is responsible for having done and what he is obligated to do as a result. By our interpretation Smith is *causally* responsible for an act normally defined as obligating, and therefore it should fall to him to satisfy whatever requirements the obligation may entail. In holding that an agent is *causally* responsible for something, we imply performance or nonperformance on his part: what he has done, is doing, or has failed to do. The latter simply means that one can be causally responsible not only for committing certain acts but for omitting them as well. When we state that Smith is obligated by the act of borrowing, his obligation is due to an act committed; but one may also be obligated by acts which are to be avoided, acts defined as undesirable by moral or legal institutions and being so defined obligate us not to commit them. We are morally, and for that matter legally, obligated not to murder, steal, commit perjury, or interfere with the civil liberties of others. Again, the obligation may be prima facie, for it is conceivable that exempting considerations could apply, as would be true for certain cases of self-defense, or taking food to prevent starvation; but our concern is not to argue what would be obligatory and why in various cases, simply to point out a definite feature of those acts generally considered obligating: namely, certain ones obligate a future performance when committed, while others involve our obligation not to commit them.

If the concepts of responsibility and obligation are related in the manner just described, then other questions must be considered. First, how much can be assumed from knowing that an agent is responsible for an obligating act? Is responsibility in the present sense a sufficient condition for concluding either the nature of an agent's obligation or whether it is his to satisfy? This seems doubtful for a number of reasons. One of the more obvious is that relevant variations in a normally expected course of events could negate its satisfaction. The classic example from Plato is appropriate: though an implicit promise has been made, should Smith honor the resulting obligation under all conditions, regardless of whatever outcome seems likely?[2] Suppose the item could be used as a weapon and his friend, after a heated argument with someone, comes to him in an obvious state of anger demanding his property. Should Smith satisfy the original obligation when it now requires him to perform a second act which he believes will lead directly to the injury of another person? Fulfilling the obligation under these conditions seems unjustified from a moral point of view, and there are grounds for stating that an opposite course of action should be taken. This would not mean that Smith is free to keep the item, that he is no longer or in any way obligated to return it, but rather that he is not obligated to do so in every conceivable situation, especially those where exempting factors occur and ought to be considered.

Numerous examples can be given to demonstrate that what seems an obvious obligation at one point in time—e.g., to keep a promise, to tell the truth, or even to obey certain laws—can later appear quite undesirable morally, given the interposition of unforeseen and morally significant factors. On these occasions points of view as to what is obligatory and why could vary depending on the ethical theory, principles or beliefs applied, and several have been discussed extensively by philosophers. Though it will serve little purpose to summarize them here, it is important to outline the position we shall assume: that an agent is *causally* responsible for an act initially obligating him to some future performance is not, in itself, a sufficient condition for concluding that he will remain obligated. We shall follow Ross,[3] Brant,[4] and others to the extent of making a distinction between an agent's prima facie obligation to do something as a result of having committed an obligating act, and what his overall obligation would be after considering other relevant factors. Prima facie obligations would hold in the absence of any factors supporting an exception to what they require, and on those occasions we would say the agent's overall obligation is the same.

But there is a further reason why a mere instance of responsibility is insufficient grounds for concluding either the content of an obligation or its proper assignment. An agent might be responsible for an act that was intentional or unintentional, individual or corporate, and extending to include primary and secondary results, all of which could affect the ultimate obligation involved. Again, consider the manufacturing concern marketing a product containing a fairly toxic substance. A primary result could be that the product functions well in terms of its intended purpose; a secondary result could be that it is later discovered to be associated with cases of poisoning. Though the firm is casually responsible for the product, marketing it with an undesirable ingredient may have been intentional or unintentional, the decision to market it a corporate or perhaps individual one, and the firm might eventually be considered responsible not only for the product's existence—and so be asked to remove it from the market—but also for its consequences.

If injury or death occurs and damages are claimed, conditions of an obligation for reparative settlement probably would vary depending on the extent of the injury and how aware the company was of the product's potential hazard, the degree of culpability being a function of both. If the firm is incorporated, it also is likely that the obligation would be assigned to the firm itself rather than to any particular person. Should this be the case, the requirements imposed by the obligation would have to be shared by persons who were not causally responsible for the product's formulation, marketing, or eventual results, e.g., stockholders through lower dividends or consumers through higher prices to offset the penalty. In effect, they would be making restitution because of acts which are the causal responsibility of others—in this instance, corporate employees—while the latter would be in the position of being able to transfer the reparative obligations they have created.

Admittedly, by virtue of their financial support, stockholders and consumers do help to make possible a corporation's existence and some may wish to contend they are causally responsible if for no other than this reason. But, at best, this argument is meaningful only to the extent that such individuals (1) possess knowledge about the decisions in question and/or their implications or (2) have decision-making powers, that is, some voice in company matters.

The second possibility does involve causal responsibility through direct participation. The first really involves level of cognizance. If a stockholder is aware that the company in which he has a financial interest engages in activities highly suspect from a moral or legal standpoint, as would be true where extreme exploitation of labor or illegal markets are known to exist, and in spite of such knowledge he continues his financial support, it would appear that he is in some way responsible. But under these circumstances what he is causally responsible for is failing to divest himself of such an association, for continuing to support activities which he knows will harm others, even though he is not directly responsible for the decisions and actions by which these activities have been set into motion. But how far can we really carry this position? What if conditions 1 and 2 do not apply? Thousands invest in the financial markets unaware of the myriad decisions and outcomes that are a daily occurrence in a complex economy, and without having direct influence on them.

There is an interesting parallel in the relationship between a person holding political office and the constituents who put him there. Are we to maintain that because certain voters are responsible for electing a president they are causally responsible for whatever actions he takes? That if he violates the public trust or commits illegal acts, these acts are theirs by virtue of their support for the man who has committed them? Granted, they are responsible for voting and in this respect are responsible for a man being in office who may later be accused of being dishonest or incompetent, but the acts which underlie a charge of dishonesty are his acts, resting on powers of decision and execution which are his and far beyond the general voter. Of course, an exception would be cases where an individual or particular group gave financial support to a candidate with the understanding that favors would be granted in return once the office was secured. This constitutes complicity, a liaison between the officeholder and those seeking favor regarding an act mutually understood, but not understood by many other persons whose responsibility extended only to the point of supporting what they considered to be a legitimate candidacy.

We can hold the foregoing position without assuming that either the general voter or others in government would be absolved of all *subsequent* responsibility, for, given an awareness of incompetence, illegal, or unethical conduct on the part of a president, they would then become responsible for the actions they take or fail to take in light of such information. What these cases illustrate is that an agent can be: (1) causally responsible for an act which is prima facie and ultimately personally obligating; (2) causally responsible for an act which is initially but not ultimately obligating because of mitigating considerations; (3) jointly responsible for an act incurring a shared obligation among those responsible; and (4) individually or jointly responsible for an act obligating others as well. Now if it is possible for an agent to be obligated by the acts of others, this would appear to weaken our thesis that responsibility is a necessary condition for attributing an obligation to any agent. It begs the question to argue that causal responsibility does exist, but that it happens to belong to agents other than the obligated.

The problem is not insurmountable if we acknowledge another sense of responsibility, one essentially noncausal in reference. An individual can have responsibilities which originate from the particular roles or positions he holds in life. It is appropriate here to say that a person has *responsibilities to* his family, community or profession; that he is *responsible for* the welfare of his children. Though many roles acquired in life can be traced to decisions for which we are causally responsible,— e. g., the decision to become a parent, the acts of procreation or adoption which bring this role about,—the present sense of the term is noncausal, since what is implied are various expectations of an individual based on the role itself. It is proper to use the phrase, *responsible for* here as well, but with this difference. When we say that Smith is "responsible for" such and such in the *causal* sense of the term, we are more concerned with actual performance or nonperformance on his part what he has done, is doing, or has failed to do; whereas, in saying that Smith is "responsible for" such and such in the *expectational* sense of the term, we imply the existence of certain acts which Smith is expected to perform or avoid, acts defined as responsibilities which he is assumed to have by virtue of having acquired a particular status and which would be expected of anyone occupying a similar position.

There are several points that need to be made about each of these meanings and their relationship to obligation. First, responsibilities falling under the expectational category can be specific or general in application. There are those specific to our work that define what it is we do; consequently, those we associate with such things as teaching, managing a plant, representing a client or holding office, responsibilities that are identified with and expected of persons occupying such positions. Other responsibilities are more general in terms of the public over which they extend and could be associated with such things as what it means to be a citizen, neighbor or member of an organization.

Second, it is clear that an agent generally has responsibilities falling into both categories. If we say that a parent is responsible for his children, we do imply causal responsibility for whatever actions or decisions he may personally effect relative to their welfare, but we also imply expectational responsibilities normally associated with being a parent, embracing events over which he may have little or no control, from a causal standpoint. This is exemplified by the case of a son, of minor age, taking the family car for the evening. Though an accident might occur for which the son is causally responsible and his parents are not, it is generally understood that their responsibility extends beyond the home, beyond conditions and periods of close proximity, to include such an event. Sharing the burden of responsibility for personal acts is part of the essence of what it means to be a juvenile or the parent of one; and so the son may have to "answer" for his driving, while his parents answer for some of its consequences.

Third, the preceding indicates that both dimensions of responsibility are directly related in a manner discussed earlier. If a person is said to have responsibilities associated with his various roles as a parent, neighbor or employee, he would be causally responsible through the omission or commission of acts tending toward their satisfaction or nonfulfillment. Citizenship involves responsibilities beyond the act of voting, e. g., to be informed about public matters and sufficiently concerned about one's government and way of life to be actively interested. A citizen would be causally responsible for satisfying or not satisfying the expectations normally associated with this role. Similarly, there are responsibilities unique to public office which are acquired and expected of persons who attain the position. Consequently, it is perfectly consistent to maintain that while congressmen may not be causally responsible for the actions of a president, they are for their own, and this would include whatever actions they take or fail to take regarding any conduct of a president constitutionally subject to their review. The stockholders in our former example were not causally responsible for the decisions and actions that created a hazardous product, but as stockholders they are owners of the corporation, and it is in this capacity that they may have to share in meeting an obligation to make restitution.

Fourth, though an agent's responsibility for an act has been contrasted with the obligations that may result, certain applications of this term closely parallel those of obligation. In the former example, it would not be uncommon to say, "Smith has a responsibility to his friend" meaning, "Smith has an obligation to his friend." Or, of a parent, that he has certain responsibilities to his children, intending that he has certain obligations to them. This usage presents little difficulty as long as we recognize that the expectational responsibilities associated with any given role constitute a justification for innumerable obligations that arise in the course of fulfilling it; in this respect the former are logically antecedent and in their implications are not always synonymous with particular obligations. If members of Congress have an obligation or a responsibility to take some form of action regarding a president, they would be obligated not only because particular circumstances seem to warrant such action, but because it is a responsibility of their office to do so.

When the term *responsibility* is used to imply an obligation, it can differ from the stricter, causal sense of the term as well. Whether the judgment is correct that Smith is causally responsible for the act of borrowing is pretty much a matter of whether a connection exists and can be established between Smith and the act in question, the relevant considerations being essentially empirical in nature. In other words, did Smith actually borrow something? This is not completely true for the second usage; empirical considerations are important to be sure, but when it is alleged that Smith has a responsibility to his friend, meaning an obligation to him, both terms can apply only if certain laws, principles, or conventions define his circumstantial status to be obligating and outline its content. In the absence of exempting conditions, similar to those noted earlier, we would probably say that Smith *ought* to return the item, that he *should* honor his obligation to do so. This language is no longer descriptive but prescriptive, and necessarily requires that we bring in normative as well as empirical considerations to justify the judgments of which it is a part.

Fifth, as a spouse or parent an agent will have responsibilities to his family, as an employee to his work, employers and colleagues. If he is active in community affairs he may have responsibilities to persons and groups involved in these same affairs. Satisfying the requirements of certain responsibilities may conflict with others, as would be true where those outside the home or to one's profession are given a degree of attention which prevents meeting those normally associated with having a family. In meeting our responsibilities and obligations we are often required to establish priorities on the basis of what is thought to be preferable, right, or of greatest worth or necessity.

It is difficult to see how an obligation can be incurred without presuming one of these forms of responsibility, and we shall regard the establishment of responsibility to be a validating condition necessary to justify the assignment of any obligation, including the obligation to be accountable. With respect to the latter, what must be demonstrated is a connection between the matters in question and the persons or agents who are expected to be answerable in their regard. The concept of responsibility is such a connection and again requires *causally*—an act actually committed, influenced, or omitted by the agent; and *expectationally*—a potential act or performance, that is (1) possible to fulfill, (2) consistent with the role from which it is said to derive, and (3) reasonable to expect in light of other considerations that are equally relevant.

Admittedly, establishing responsibility is sometimes difficult, yet it is important to be as clear as possible about *who* is responsible for *what* where an obligation is concerned. In cases of criminal accusation more than one person has gone to prison because they were mistakenly identified and held responsible for criminal acts they did not commit.

The requirements outlined in regard to expectational responsibilities are equally important. Relative to (2), we might argue that brainwashing, indoctrination, and falsifying facts or the truth should not be considered responsibilities of an educator or a scientist since they represent activities inconsistent with what it means to teach, to be educated or to follow scientific procedure. Requirement (1) implies that if an agent's responsibility centers on an expected performance and the parties expecting it wittingly or unwittingly effect conditions precluding its satisfaction, or if the possibility of its satisfaction is remote from the outset due to factors beyond the agent's power to rectify, then the expectation in that instance is unreasonable, lacks point or at least is of questionable validity. Criterion (3) simply acknowledges the complexity of life. Many responsibilities, obligations and expectations seem justified and reasonable in the beginning but eventually have to be modified because other considerations come to light which are relevant and prove to be equally if not more important.

While these conditions represent minimum prerequisites for attributing responsibility, their observance is especially important in relationships where the term *responsibility* takes on still another meaning. We refer to the distinction between being responsible for an act in either of the interpretations presented and being *held responsible* for it, where the latter implies being accountable in its regard.

Responsibility and accountability: related—but not synonymous

Several considerations explain the general tendency to equate the meaning of responsibility with that of accountability. First, the locutions "responsible for" and "accountable for" are conveniently parallel, and substituting one for the other is not incompatible with everyday usage. A school official might say to a teacher, "You are responsible for your students," intending, "You are accountable for your students"; or he might state that he is "responsible to" him, meaning "accountable to" him where they are concerned. Here, being responsible for something literally means being held accountable for it.

Second, numerous responsibilities are acknowledged for which individuals are generally thought to be accountable, assuming for the present we mean by accountable being "subject to giving an account" or "being answerable." Parents are responsible for their children and accountable to the extent that they may have to answer for neglect of basic needs or behavior which is morally or physically detrimental. Excessive punishment or contributing to a child's delinquency or ill-health through willful negligence exemplify these conditions.

As noted earlier, we have responsibilities associated with our work that define what it is we do and for which we may be subject to giving an account to persons in higher position. However, that these concepts are not entirely equivalent is evident in the fact that there are many responsibilities for which people are not accountable. Parents may be answerable in the sense indicated above, but they only have to answer in cases where behavior toward children is sufficiently unacceptable to warrant some form of social intervention; normally, parental latitude in the matter of raising children is considerable. To say that a parent is responsible for a child's welfare implies more than simply meeting basic needs; it implies that whenever *possible* an effort should be made to do whatever is in a child's best interest. Fulfillment of the latter may require that a parent assist a child in gaining certain experiences through travel, education and other forms of enrichment, or that he assist his child in acquiring proper attitudes toward himself and others. Yet however important the preceding may seem, parents are seldom held accountable for contributing to their children's prejudice, refusing to aid in their attainment of a higher education or for otherwise failing to enrich their lives.[5]

The fact that responsibility may exist without the necessary implication of accoutability is well illustrated by major institutions having numerous responsibilities extending to employees, consumers and the general public. While their fulfillment is often encouraged by a system of requirements which make the institution "answerable" for certain of its affairs—e. g., corporations must give an accounting to the government and stockholders concerning fiscal matters—they too enjoy considerable discretion and have responsibilities for which they are not always accountable. One could argue that since their existence depends to a certain degree on natural resources and a consumer public, special responsibilities exist not to engage in practices harmful to either; that, where avoidable, there is a responsibility not to exploit resources or to produce goods whose composition and use may be injurious to the public. Yet it is a matter of record that some corporations have been avoidably and directly responsible for actions similar to these and have been held unaccountable in doing so.

The point is that satisfaction of the foregoing conditions for establishing responsibility would permit us to maintain an agent's responsibility for a given act without implying that he is necessarily accountable for it. Accountability is by no means a necessary consequence of responsibility, and, as we shall argue, there are occasions when it should not be made to be. But surely the reverse does not follow. If an agent *is* to be accountable, he must be accountable for something; and to hold him responsible for an act in this sense of the term presupposes some connection on his part with the act or state of affairs for which he must answer. Therefore, these conditions should be satisfied and the responsibility they establish clearly demonstrated where such a relationship exists or is demanded. In alleging that their satisfaction is prerequisite to any obligation, we mean just that, and include the obligation to account as well as others that may be incurred. It is highly questionable whether an agent should be held accountable for acts or performances which causally he has neither omitted, committed, or influenced; or for expected performances which are impossible to satisfy, are inconsistent with the role from which they are said to derive, or whose assignment and satisfaction may be quite unjustified by other factors. Moreover, it is questionable whether an agent should be held solely accountable for matters involving a shared, causal responsibility, or for expected performances requiring a shared influence, unless it is specifically understood that the agent is answerable for the actions of others, as would seem to be true of a parent or an executive responsible for the work of subordinates.

Entitlement: the second validating condition

We have taken the position that establishing an agent's responsibility is a necessary condition for validating his or her obligation to be accountable, but there are other factors which influence the validity and effectiveness of such relationships. First, there is the matter of which institutions actually define particular acts, performances, or responsibilities to be obligating; that is, provide additional grounds for saying that where this responsibility is concerned the agent should give an account. For the present we shall assume that the institutional basis for any obligation must be (a) moral, (b) legal, or (c) a concurrence of the two.[6] It is acknowledged that in regard to a moral obligation, interpretations of whether or not an agent is obligated would depend partly on (1) the particular theory of moral obligation one assumes—whether, for example, the theory of voluntary action is essentially deontological or teleological in view; or, in the absence of (1), (2) the prevailing morality or customs of a people, and (3) the various circumstantial considerations that may be relevant to an agent's overall obligation on any occasion.

Second, there is the problem of entitlement. If an agent is to be accountable, not only must he be accountable for matters in relation to which he is justifiably responsible, but he also would have to be accountable to someone—to other parties who, by virtue of some manner of entitlement, are to receive the account rendered. On what grounds such entitlement rests would surely have a bearing on whether particular demands for accountability are justified.

The significance of the institutions which define an obligation to account, and the entitlement of those who might expect it, can be illustrated if we consider the situation of a wife seeking a separation from her husband. In the institution of marriage we have a good example of a human relationship involving important responsibilities; on the one hand, those taking the form of conventional expectations commonly assumed of anyone entering such an arrangement; on the other, responsibilities of a more particular sort, which arise during the course of living out its mutual commitments.

In American culture marriage has traditionally been regarded as an institution of central importance to society, at least in theory if not always in practice; one not to be taken lightly either morally or legally, as evidenced in the ceremonial rituals by which it is brought into being and in the procedural conditions governing its termination. Consistency with our earlier analysis requires that where a husband or wife chooses to end this commitment, justifying reasons should exist to support their doing so.

In the present case we shall assume that reasons support the decision, e. g., on grounds of neglect, infidelity, or some form of family abuse. Significant here is the fact that requests for these reasons could come from a number of sources—close friends, neighbors, relatives, casual acquaintances, the wife's children, or her husband—but her moral obligation to respond could vary markedly. She may suspect that certain neighbors are motivated more by curiosity than by a genuine interest in her or her family's welfare; or she may believe that a premature accounting of her reasons, even to fairly close friends, will jeopardize her position, especially if litigation is to ensue. The obligation to give an account under these conditions is negligible, and differs in degree and justification from that attending similar requests from her husband and children. Given the mutual interdependence and obligations in marriage, they are entitled to an account of her reasons in a way in which the others are not, even though the explanation to her children may be substantially different from that given to her husband. Where neighbors and casual acquaintances are involved, we might even agree that the separation and reasons behind it are really "none of their business" and not be too surprised if this were her response to their persistence in seeking an account. But it would be strange, indeed, if she announced to her husband her intention of leaving and when asked to give her reasons replied that it was none of *his* business.

Though consistency requires that we recognize or attribute an obligation on every occasion having the same characteristics, the fact remains that our obligation to satisfy various demands for an account will often vary and do so according to a variety of considerations relevant to the occasion of such demands. Certainly, the question of entitlement is one of them. If an obligation to account must rest on some demonstrable connection between the accounting agent and the state of affairs for which he is answerable, it seems reasonable to make a similar condition where the matter of entitlement is concerned. To require that parties soliciting the account have a definite connection or valid interest in the affairs it is about, and that this interest be something more than curiosity. Prima facie, taxpayers have an interest in how their taxes are spent, parents in how their children are treated, and, under democratic forms of social organization, those governed in how they are governed. What must be demonstrated, then, is that the matter of their concern relates significantly to their lives, and that their claim to an account is supported by this consideration together with the dictates of moral or legal reasoning.

At the same time, we have no reason to suppose that those having such an interest would always be restricted in number or that the forms of accounting to which they feel entitled would always be similar. The problem of entitlement is particularly difficult in relationships of accountability since agents demanding an accounting may differ in the degree of their entitlement, necessitating priority relationships, differ in the forms of accounting they expect, the reasons why they expect them, and the criteria by which they judge their adequacy. Despite these considerations we shall maintain that entitlement is a function of whether a legitimate interest can be shown by those expecting an account in whatever affairs it concerns, and that this condition must be met to validate an obligation to satisfy an accountability demand. We recognize the husband's entitlement because of the contractual nature of marriage, the mutual obligations contractual arrangements involve, and because there are moral grounds implying that any person who has an intimate and prolonged relationship of this nature would be entitled to know the reasons why it is to be altered.

The grounds for accountability in education

Two elements central to the concept of accountability and its application have been identified: (1) various methods or forms of accounting, and (2) the obligation to account validated by the conditions of agent responsibility and entitlement. Both elements provide grounds for accountability in education. On the one hand, we noted that the various forms of accounting described in chapter 1 are primary tools of communication, indispensable to rational procedure, and that because of this role their development must be included among the central aims of education. Viewed from this perspective, schools have a responsibility to provide experiences that will assist students to become more adept at accounting for themselves and for those responsibilities in life about which others may justifiably inquire. By the completion of their schooling we assume that students should be skilled in these forms of accounting, competent in relating information and reporting events, in explaining their ideas and reasons for things, and in justifying their actions.

On the other hand, we have taken the position that "responsibility" and "entitlement" are necessary conditions for the assignment of any accountability obligation, and that in this capacity both serve as a foundation for accountability relationships. It is our contention that people should not be held accountable for matters in relation to which they have neither a causal nor an expectational responsibility; and, further, that where their responsibility can be demonstrated, an obligation to be accountable in its regard would be justified only where those expecting it have such entitlement by virtue of their relationship to the matter or persons in question.

These conditions which must obtain to establish valid obligations of accountability on other spheres of human activity have a similar role in the field of education. There are, after all, few endeavors which involve a set of responsibilities more serious from both a moral and a legal point of view than the formal education of children. There is the responsibility of choosing which ends and objectives of education to pursue, and the responsibility of selecting methods of instruction which are appropriate in terms of the treatment of children and which are educationally sound in promoting the attainment of such ends once chosen. In our society, the goals and processes of education are considered important enough to be embodied within elaborate institutional structures where experiencing them is required by law and directed over many years of a child's life. To deliberately set about to change a person, toward goals and utilizing methods over which they have little say or latitude of choice, is an undertaking involving major responsibilities to say the least.

But there are entitlements in education as well. Under the law parents may have little choice in the general matter of whether or not their children will experience some form of education, but most persons would agree that parents are entitled to inquire about the welfare of their children. They have a right to know about their children's progress and treatment in school, and, as citizens and taxpayers, they have a right to inquire about school policies and the expenditure of school funds. Because of their role, school committee members are entitled to an accounting from school administrators and faculty concerning student programs, fiscal policies and other matters of legitimate concern in the operation of schools under their jurisdiction. Our point is simply that by its nature formal education is an undertaking involving both of these conditions, where rights and significant responsibilities can be readily identified, and for this reason it is a field in which accountability relationships will necessarily feature.

In summary, we have outlined two conditions necessary to establish obligations of accountability and the requirements they may impose: (1) a demonstrated responsibility on the part of an agent in relation to the matters for which he or she is considered answerable—this condition establishes *who* is accountable; and (2) a clear entitlement to some form of accounting because the matters in question bear significantly on the interests of those who expect it. This condition establishes which parties may justifiably receive or expect an account and hence is necessary to validate an agent's obligation to give it. Accountability obligations are defined and established on the basis of other factors which are equally important, but before they can be examined we must deal with a major challenge to the position we have taken concerning "responsibility" and its role in validating accountability relationships. The challenge to our thesis stems from basic assumptions underlying the theory of operant-conditioning. B. F. Skinner and his followers essentially contend that behavior is entirely shaped by our environment and the prior conditioning of one's past. People may operate under the assumption that they have some choice in what they do, but in reality their behavior is predetermined by factors beyond their control; consequently, people are not responsible for their actions. The concepts of free choice and responsibility are basically prescientific notions which continue to survive because of ignorance or a stubborn refusal to accept principles of behavior that have evolved from years of research in the field of behavioral science. The degree to which this theory may be valid and the extent to which it is accepted as the only explanation for human behavior obviously carry serious implications for the concept of accountability and its application. After all, if people are not responsible for their behavior, what point or justification can there be in holding them accountable for their actions, or for that matter for consequences which we attribute to decisions they have made? In the following chapter we shall analyze several assumptions associated with this theory, and in the process prepare the way for a discussion of the moral and legal dimensions of accountability.

CHAPTER 4

Responsibility and the problem of determinism

Several motivational strategies employed by performance contractors were criticized in the second chapter, but we also acknowledged a body of research in the area of operant conditioning, recognizing the fact that most people are motivated to greater achievement when their behavior is positively reinforced. However, whether these strategies should be used is a more fundamental issue than our initial concern that they be used with care and a sensible perspective concerning their role and ultimate value. Simply stated, our analysis of accountability runs counter to the theory of operant conditioning which provides the basis for such techniques. The latter is fundamentally opposed to the idea that people are responsible for their behavior or that from a causal standpoint there are any responsibilities for which people ought to be accountable. In Skinner's view, whatever our achievements or failings may seem to be, they clearly are not matters for which we are responsible, if this is taken to imply that they are the result of free choice or autonomous behavior on our part. Rather, our behavior is determined and shaped by the environment in which it occurs and, more importantly, by the consequences which attend it. In acknowledging the contributions of Pavlov, Skinner stresses that operant conditioning involves more than simple stimulus-response theory:

> When Pavlov showed how new reflexes could be built up through conditioning, a full-fledged stimulus-response psychology was born, in which all behavior was regarded as reactions to stimuli. One writer put it this way: "We are prodded or lashed through life." The stimulus-response model was never very convincing, however . . . The environment not only prods or lashes, it *selects*. Its role is similar to that in natural selection, though on a very different time scale . . . It is now clear that we must take into account what the environment does to an organism not only before but after it responds. Behavior is shaped and maintained by its consequences.[1]

For our purposes, two challenges are presented by the conclusions which Skinner and his colleagues have drawn from their research. First, operant conditioning is not offered as a theory to explain a part or, for that matter, even key elements of behavior; on the contrary, it is considered sufficient as an explanation for all of human behavior. According to this school of thought, whatever our behavior may be at any given moment, it is *totally* the result of operant conditioning, the culmination of years of contingencies conditioning and modifying behavior as we move through life in constant interaction with our environment. Each behavioral action, however momentary or complex, represents a highly predictable resultant, an endpoint which is invariant and entirely predetermined by the conditioning which has taken place prior to the instant when it occurs. People may deliberate and feel that they have a choice in what they do, but in reality what they do is already determined by their past. Furthermore, our behavior at any given moment is so firmly determined by our past that if operant-conditioning scientists could know our entire behavioral history and be given a complete picture of our present situation, it is assumed they could predict with a high degree of certainty what our next act or decision would be. In *Beyond Freedom and Dignity* Skinner stresses that concepts such as responsibility, personal autonomy and freedom of choice are nothing more than vacuous notions left over from ages of prescientific thinking. The implications of the foregoing for a theory of accountability are clear. How can we hold people accountable for what they do when all of their actions really are not of their choosing, but instead derive from control mechanisms completely external to themselves?

Despite the foregoing, all is not lost: In Skinner's view, behavior can be changed and altered for the better. The second challenge to our analysis of accountability involves two other conclusions from operant-conditioning research; both establish a basis for changing behavior and provide the underlying rationale for behavior modification strategies:

> One concerns the basic analysis. Behavior which operates upon the environment to produce consequences ('operant' behavior) can be studied by arranging environments in which specific consequences are contingent upon it. The contingencies under investigation have become steadily more complex, and one by one they are taking over the explanatory functions previously assigned to personalities, states of mind, feelings, traits of character, purposes and intentions. The second result is practical: the environment can be manipulated. It is true that man's genetic endowment can be changed only very slowly, but changes in the environment of the individual have quick and dramatic effects.[2]

In essence, proponents of this theory reject the position that we can be direct agents in changing our behavior through internal mechanisms involving traits of character, reasoning, and ultimately by making what we believe to be a rational and personal choice. Since the conditions which control behavior reside within the environment, if we wish to change the behavior of an individual, our efforts must be directed at changing the environment in which he or she operates rather than at trying to change the person by an appeal to personal attributes or internal dispositions which we erroneously assume him or her to have.

The real issue is the effectiveness of techniques of control. We shall not solve the problems of alcoholism and juvenile delinquency by increasing a sense of responsibility. It is the environment which is 'responsible' for the objectionable behavior, and it is the environment, not some attribute of the individual, which must be changed.[3]

The implications of this theory for a concept of accountability are serious to say the least, but if its basic precepts are accepted as an adequate explanation for behavior, the implications go far beyond accountability, clearly undermining basic assumptions and principles which define the purpose and structure of many social institutions. As Gaylin observed, Skinner rejects most if not all major assumptions associated with law, religion, anthropology, psychotherapy, psychology, philosophy, ethics, education, political science, and history on the grounds that these fields are unscientific in their view of human behavior and, consequently, in error regarding the theoretical foundations on which they are based.

Of course, the primary question is whether operant conditioning is sufficient as an explanation for behavior, or whether the realities of history and our existence suggest other possibilities. Understandably, we believe that they do or this study of accountability would not have been undertaken. But the problem posed by Skinner's thesis is not so easily resolved. First, as an explanation for why people behave as they do, it cannot be dismissed out of hand, as some proponents of alternative theories would have us believe. The debatable issue cannot be framed on the question "Is Skinner's thesis correct or incorrect?" In truth, the difficulty lies in the fact that Skinner is correct about much of our behavior—we *do* behave on the basis of prior conditioning, and much of our behavior is modified by an environment that is reinforcing and sometimes negative in its responses to what we do. This generally is the case within the environment where people work. Although the environmental contexts of work vary considerably for individuals, many components are similar. Most of us work for and must report to someone in a higher position than our own; what we do is supervised and based on job functions designed around institutional requirements and the expectations of others. The reinforcements we receive often are in the form of rewards such as a paycheck, bonuses, a smile or occasional praise. On the other hand, if we are negligent or show poor performance in meeting expectations, we may be reprimanded or experience other punitive measures. Without question, our actions are influenced by positive reinforcement and by responses that can be negative or reflect indifference. But because operant conditioning can account for much of our behavior, it does not follow that it is sufficient to explain all of it. While it is not the primary purpose of this study to offer an extensive analysis of Skinner's thesis, more is required than simply saying Skinner is wrong if our position on accountability is to be creditable. The remainder of this chapter will be devoted to exploring several problems associated with operant conditioning which we contend seriously limit the ability of this theory to address many problems and issues that are a part of everyday life. Given the extremely deterministic conception of behavior espoused by this theory, the associated methods and strategies which it advocates and the thrust of Skinner's criticisms regarding most institutions concerned with influencing or interpreting human behavior, it is clear that more is at issue than the concept of accountability.

Operant conditioning and the element of choice

From the standpoint of accountability, two basic problems are posed by this theory. First, there is the issue of whether or not we have any freedom of choice, or whether our behavior is entirely driven by the environmental responses it produces and modified only by external factors. Stated differently, do we have *any,* or for that matter *enough,* latitude of choice to be in some sense responsible for any of the things we do? And, second, can the degree of choice we may have on any given occasion be sufficient to preclude the absolute level of predictability that behaviorists seem to assume? Although quite simple, Gaylin provides an example which focuses on the issue of personal choice and the problem of predicting behavior.

Let me offer an example: A man is five pounds overweight and he has just decided that he will stop all snacks for the next month. It is the first night of this resolve. He is seated at a dinner meeting, listening to a rather dull lecture on freedom and determinism. The waiter places in front of him a bowl of peanuts, a particular weakness of our would-be dieter. Within ten seconds, the subject has an impulse to take a peanut. The question is simply to predict whether he will take the peanut or not at the time of that first impulse. Obviously, no one of the scientific mind would accept this test case and make a prediction. There are too many variables which are unknown to determine this particular piece of behavior. It is no different from being given a complex problem in physics with incomplete data. We simply could not know.

Now let us examine the next step. You are given the data that he does not follow the impulse. He does not take the peanut. Without analyzing the variables, you know that an entire lifetime of complex inputs toward taking the peanut have been placed on one side of the scale and an entire lifetime of training and conditioning to resist the peanut are added to the other side of the scale. We are asked to believe that, given that particular individual, that particular lifetime, and those particular conditions, at that particular moment of time, the refusal of the peanut was predetermined, in precisely the same way as if balancing weights were added to one side or the other. You are then told that three seconds later he has a second impulse. You now have the great advantage of knowing that an entire lifetime of inputs and variables, whether knowable or not, have culminated in the first decision to resist the impulse. Are you now prepared to predict the response to the second impulse?

You are not. Even though you start with the resultant of the immense number of seconds before the first decision and all you have to balance against that is three insignificant seconds of time. And if I were to give you the pattern of fifty impulses leading both to acceptance and rejection, you would be no better off predicting the fifty-first even if the interval were reduced to one-tenth of a second. For the number of variables that could be introduced in that fraction of time are as incalculable as those in that mass of time preceding the first decision. The same is not true of weights and measures, and that is what makes prediction of human behavior different from prediction of the behavior of inanimate things or of simple animal forms. Whether that is truly a "free" choice or not, it is an incalculable choice, and as such can pass for freedom.[4]

Gaylin acknowledges the fact that a man can be conditioned to resist peanuts, but is quick to point out that his example has little or nothing to do with peanuts. "It is concerned with impulse and control, passion and reason, appetite and knowledge, pleasure and safety, rationalization and rationality, hunger and wants, instinct and learning, motives and counter-motives, thought and action—and the complexity of the human mind, which in denying predictability, defies programming."[5] We concur with the foregoing, but with a slightly different interpretation. In denying the predictability which behaviorists would claim, these elements suggest that human behavior functions as the result of a complexity of inputs, some of which are internal to ourselves and as much a part of our total existence as the external world and environment in which we live; but although these internal factors can militate against programming behavior, they do not preclude the possibility. Media advertisements offer a good example of how knowledge about the conditions which govern human insecurity, want and desire can be wedded to systematic strategies for conditioning behavior to promote ends and sometimes purposes designed to serve the interests of others. The fact is we can be programmed, and often are, to the extent that other people may have such knowledge and the position to manipulate and control the environment in which we live.

The NAZI Youth Corps in Germany illustrates the power which environmental manipulation and operant conditioning can have over the individual, particularly at an impressionable age. To reiterate a claim by Skinner, our use of this example is not meant to be pejorative. It simply is a fact that scores of German youth were turned from family ties and allegiances to follow a regime which capitalized on their natural subservience to adult power and authority. By exploiting a need for structure and a feeling of significance, and by using reinforcements in the form of medals, uniforms and recognition, authorities in the Nazi movement influenced many youth to obey and become willing servants for the cause, even to the point of denying family and friends. Let there be no doubt, the behavior of people can be conditioned and modified to the desires of others, whether the others are a government, a teenage peer group or parents. Children are not born racist; their beliefs, whether right or wrong, good or bad, often are acquired and become settled through a reinforcement and conditioning process that takes place within the contexts of their dependence.

We empathize with the man in Gaylin's example, well intentioned in his goal to lose five pounds; but others would find this a trifling example against years of research in the behaviorist laboratory. However, it was selected because much of Skinner's research and that of his followers is very similar. On the surface, how much difference is there between food pellets for the rat and peanuts for a man? Perhaps little for the behaviorist, but a great deal as far as we are concerned. Gaylin is eloquent in identifying elements of our world and personal nature which do impinge on our behavior, however momentary their incursion into the stream of our experience and behavior may be, to set us apart from such easy predictability. Given the power of environmental conditioning already conceded, even Skinner must acknowledge that the potential variables that could come into play prior to our subject's response to his impulse, if not infinite, are sufficient in number to defy comprehension, largely because of the mind, the power to reflect, to consider if only for an instant any number of a thousand possible thoughts.

Externally, there is the matter of reflex and our subject's response to distraction. Suppose the waiter spills a glass of wine in his lap a split second after his second impulse to take a peanut. Very likely, the behaviorist would persist in his position that if he knew all of the circumstances, including this accident, then our subject's behavior could be accurately predicted. But the challenge to the behaviorist is considerable, for he must, on the grounds of operant conditioning, predict whether or not our subject would or would not follow his impulse in taking the peanut after the introduction of a momentary and split-second variable; and the behaviorist must deal with the issue of our subject's response to the accident itself, e. g., whether or not he would be gracious, angry or indifferent to the waiter because of the accident, quite apart from whether or not our subject follows his initial impulse.

In everyone's life, distractions are commonplace. If our subject fails to follow his impulse, would this be the result of prior conditioning or of simply being momentarily distracted? And were the accident and the distraction themselves predetermined by conditioning? We think not. In human relationships the nuances of physical and verbal communication may be regarded as part of the environment, but these forms of exchange between people often are very subtle and instantaneous, evoking responses to be expected as well as responses quite unexpected. For this reason it is doubtful that even the observable context could be completely understood and predicted. We doubt that the waiter spilled the drink because he was conditioned to do so. He slipped or for an instant misjudged his perception in reaching for the glass, perhaps because he was momentarily distracted; but his reaction to the event could be equally difficult to predict, depending upon his mood, present thoughts, perhaps his fatigue and, yes, even his "feelings" at the time. The waiter may act indifferent, showing little concern for the inconvenience and discomfort he has caused, prompting impatience or anger in our subject; or through his general manner, facial expressions, "body language" and comments he may appear to be distressed and genuinely sorry. These behavioral reflections could be very subtle and momentary, but nevertheless occasion in our subject some identity with the waiter's plight, an immediate empathy which comes from recognition, perhaps at the edge of the subconscious, of what it is to make a mistake and to be embarrassed when one has done something which makes one vulnerable, diminishing one's pride and sense of worth—and in the empathy of that moment, our subject may act graciously despite his discomfort, or he may not. Within such situations, actions of communication can occur rapidly when events seem to rush by us with little or no time for reflection and our behavior seems to call upon simply what we are. But occasionally our reactions will surprise even ourselves, appear contrary to how we normally behave and vary from the way in which we generally see ourselves. Afterward, we may regret something we did or said, or feel satisfaction that somehow we rose to the occasion.

However simple it may appear to be, this example illustrates the complexity of human behavior, the problem of understanding and determining the factors which govern it, the degree to which the latter can be accurately predicted, and whether the expected and predictable can be altered by unforseen events. Operant-conditioning theorists ignore the present context in its entirety, not only the environmental context about which much can be known and described, but a context which includes the individual and all that is a part of him. A great deal of our behavior is habitual and undoubtedly the result of prior conditioning, but much of it is influenced by our mood, by the thoughts and the worries that we carry, all of which can be part of our consciousness or at the threshold of our subconscious at the time.

Given Skinner's position, there is the additional problem of altruistic behavior and how one is to view what is commonly regarded as acting from a sense of duty or meeting one's obligations. This is especially true in circumstances where personal rewards and reinforcements appear remote if at all possible, when doing something for others represents hardship and sacrifice, or the denial of what might be greater personal ease or a life more meaningful and fulfilling. Perhaps the behaviorist would say that if one person behaves altruistically toward another, it is because the former has been conditioned to do so by prior environmental contingencies, and that future environmental responses must at some point be reinforcing for the behavior to continue. A single parent working long hours at more than one job in an effort to support and keep a family together will find little comfort in this position, and it seems to beg the question. True, the reinforcement for such sacrifice may reside in the family itself, in the satisfaction one derives from mutual belonging, love and caring. But for some individuals, the determination and effort put forth in trying to provide for a family also represent convictions about meeting the responsibilities one has incurred, or they derive from a strong sense of obligation or duty. More than one parent has persisted under considerable odds, even when some of their children repeatedly have shown that they are not and likely never will be what a parent wishes or hopes them to be. Indeed, the parent's behavior may be reinforced by the dream, but the actual reinforcement can be remote to say the least; and to contend that their behavior persists because of some distant reward is simply to say that our hope for the future can drive us to continue as much as the conditioning of our past.

In discussing the history of man's achievements in the arts and sciences, Bronowski observed that Skinner wrote the books on operant conditioning and behavior modification; they were not written by pigeons or rats, nor are books likely ever to be. Again, this comment may seem pejorative, but it focuses on the heart of the issue. Skinner's theory discounts a great deal of historical evidence about the uniqueness of the human mind and spirit, especially in those who are gifted in their imagination, their creativity and their ability to perceive, to understand and ultimately to propose what others fail to see. These attributes of mind and character have been manifested throughout a long history of accomplishment in the arts and the humanities, in engineering, science, medicine, politics, the law and other areas of human endeavor. Achievements in these fields testify to the power and potential of the mind whether it is the ability to reason, to analyze and understand, to compare and make choices or the simple determination to see something through even when faced with considerable odds. Apropos of the discussion, did Skinner adopt and finally advocate his theory of human behavior only as a result of environmental contingencies and his prior conditioning, or did it also result from personal decisions along the way, decisions which also involved an element of free and independent choice? Prior conditioning may have played a part in shaping his behavior to study, to persist in inquiry, to write, and to achieve, but why this theory and not another? There must have been occasions when experiments failed and things simply did not fall into place, occasions when he and his colleagues discussed disappointing results, pondered the reasons for their failure, considered alternative possibilities and sought new approaches to the problems with which they were struggling. And when new approaches were tried, did the selected course of action result exclusively from the reinforcement associated with prior success and the behavioral inclination to avoid failure? Or were particular approaches selected because as scientists they came to terms with the evidence, speculated about alternative possibilities and on the basis of *reasoning* selected what then appeared to be the best *choice?*

Values and the issue of ethical relativism

There also is the matter of values. In arguing for a better world and the need to utilize operant-conditioning strategies to achieve desirable behavior in our youth, Dr. Skinner's values are made clear. At the time he was concerned that students no longer responded to educational environments in traditional ways, that they dropped out of school and only took courses which they enjoyed and which seemed relevant to their problems. Writing during the Vietnam War, he lamented that "young people refused to serve in the armed forces and desert or defect to other countries, but we shall not make an appreciable change by 'inspiring greater loyalty or patriotism.' What must be changed are the contingencies which induce young people to behave in given ways toward their governments."[6] These sentiments were no doubt held by the leadership of the Third Reich as they implemented strategies to induce the youth of Nazi Germany "to behave in given ways" toward their government. Undoubtedly, Skinner's concerns are well intentioned, and we imagine that he was as appalled by the total range of values associated with the Nazi movement as were many people. Nevertheless, while Skinner rejects the analytical tools and understandings which have evolved from years of study in moral and ethical theory, he advocates a theory of behavior which places him in the middle of a dilemma involving ethical relativism and simple logic. Logically, there is the contradiction in maintaining that our behavior results exclusively from prior conditioning while at the same time presenting values which he has internalized and which, for reasons unstated, he believes are sufficiently preferable to invoke major environmental change in the interest of promoting their adoption. Without question, Skinner offers a design for a better world that is clearly based on his personal convictions and values.

Now Skinner could rejoin that the values he advocates were not acquired through a process involving personal deliberation and choice, but instead were acquired as the result of conditioning, and the fact that he holds them remains consistent with his basic theory of human behavior. In other words, his values are no more the result of personal assessment and choice than the values held by other people, but were fashioned as a natural outcome of his environmental history. However, if the position is taken that this is the only means by which values can be acquired, then the same would be true of the values and beliefs associated with the Nazi movement, and Skinner is caught in the middle of an ethical as well as an empirical relativism. From an empirical standpoint, Skinner is correct—values do vary from one culture and people to another and are relative in this sense. But because a differentiated pattern of values exists among cultures, we do not have to accept the position that all values within such an empirical pattern are equally valid from a moral point of view. The basic challenge for Skinner is similar to that posed for all of us: why should we accept and subscribe to Skinner's values any more than to those promulgated by the Nazis? We hope that Skinner would concede that there are reasons to reject the values of Nazi Germany, but the reasons for rejecting them have as much to do with our judgments about human rights, our sense of what is fair and just, as they do with conditioning. Skinner's theory offers no means by which individuals or social institutions can judge the moral preference of one set of values in relation to another, nor a means to assist us in developing a better understanding of such issues. In criticizing contemporary culture and its youth, and in offering his view of what the world *ought* to be like, Skinner does so without providing a rationale for his position, yet he enters the realm of normative judgment where decisions about what ought or ought not to be necessarily involve considerations that go beyond the laboratory and what is empirically given. At issue are questions not only about how people actually do behave, but perceptions about how individuals and societies ought to behave, how they ought to treat one another and in what areas of human conduct freedom should or should not be constrained.

Responsibility and coping with everyday problems

This brings us to another limitation of this theory: Taken alone, it offers very little that can help us in dealing with the most important and perplexing problems of life, many of which are intimately connected to what we value and believe is important; nor does it account for the special considerations and the kind of normative and analytical reasoning required in solving such problems. Nowhere is this limitation more evident than in relation to the role which values and the assignment of responsibility must play in our personal lives and in the function of major social institutions.

From an individual perspective, psychiatrists' offices are filled with people who struggle with the realization that for many years their orientation to life *has been* based on values they were conditioned to accept, rather than on a set of values forged through a process involving personal reflection and choice. More than one person has acquired fame and fortune only to discover that the fulfillment and happiness they had been conditioned to believe would be associated with such achievement simply were not there. The progressive disillusionment and ultimate discovery in such situations can be disastrous, to say the least: for some this has meant drug abuse, alcoholism, shattered relationships or even death, while for others it can be a turning point, the beginning of personal introspection and a rather long and often painful search to discover what is meaningful. Interestingly, to some degree the psychoanalyst also operates on a set of deterministic assumptions about behavior. Analysis is predicated, in part, on the belief that childhood experiences establish many of the insecurities and anxieties with which one must contend in adult life; but there is a major difference between the strict determinism associated with Skinner's theory and the softer determinism of psychoanalytic theory. The latter assumes that through analysis of these earlier experiences and by a process of self-examination many people can become aware of their influence and on the basis of such awareness do something about them. In essence, the analyst assumes that however difficult the struggle may be, an individual can make a difference in the course of his or her life, that one's present and future existence is not cast in stone but can be altered, and altered through personal effort.

Furthermore, Skinner's theory appears inconsistent with the fact that, despite the context of their environment, people from all walks of life become increasingly concerned about the meaning of their existence, about the values and beliefs they hold, why they hold them and whether the latter are really adequate or meaningful in light of other possibilities. These occasions or stages in a person's life can initiate a process where individuals seek greater self-awareness with a view to changing how they live. They may strive to gain a better understanding of the "why" of things, or attempt to evolve a set of principles and beliefs that are more realistic in helping them to cope with many problems and issues with which they and others around them must deal.

There are people who do agree with Socrates that "the unexamined life is not worth living," and in their engagement with all that life presents, there are some who will strive to affect its course through personal reflection and choice and by seeking the knowledge and ideas of others. Perhaps their efforts stem from the realization that things are not as they would like them to be or that they are not as they should be; but they also derive from a personal belief that *they* can make a difference in what happens, at least some of the time. The characteristics of a rational existence discussed in the second chapter are very much involved in this orientation to life, for it is by questioning and through the exchange of ideas and reasons that we gain much of our understanding and test our convictions in relation to those held by others.

Now Skinner and his colleagues could argue that in all of this talk about reasoning and exchanging ideas with others, we forget that the others of whom we speak are really external to ourselves, and only comprise another response element in the environment. Of course this is correct, but it is not the issue. The problem is more than one of semantics; it centers on the role which human cognition and reasoning can play in this environmental—human equation and what the individual can do with the responses he or she receives. In criticizing operant-conditioning theory, we recognize that there are other psychological theories to explain behavior. Some ignore environmental conditioning altogether and focus on factors considered internal to the individual, and do so to a degree that suggests a form of inner determinism. Both extremes belie the complexity of human behavior because they operate on the basis of theoretical assumptions and premises which are too narrowly defined and which seem to be designed more in the interest of providing theoretical coherence than coming to terms with what is really presented to us in the behavior of people. Can theories which appear intrinsically coherent and yet involve major premises that are inconsistent with those of competing theories all be correct? Whether the approach taken is that of the developmentalist, the psychoanalyst or the operant-conditioning theorist, it is probably closer to the truth to recognize that each of these approaches provides some insight into behavior. The student of human behavior must discover which elements of each theory have validity and somehow assimilate these elements into a more adequate and plausible explanation. The tendency to assume that behavior must be explained by this theory or that theory often poses false dichotomies not unlike the argument over nature-versus-nurture and which of the two really determines who we are and potentially what we can become. The nature-versus-nurture dichotomy is somewhat analogous to the position adopted by Skinner in relation to other psychological theories.

Research supports the fact that biological endowment and one's genetic history are key factors in determining intellectual capacity, physical attributes, personal health and potential longevity; but research also indicates that personal experience and the environmental circumstances of one's existence are important factors as well, factors that can greatly alter the direction of a person's life and influence the realization of his or her genetic potential, whatever it may be. Genetically, a person could inherit a high degree of native intelligence, evidenced by testing or many instances of insight or creative problem solving, yet throughout life this same person could remain ignorant about many things which are common knowledge to others simply because of the limited experience and opportunities that his or her environment may have imposed. Nature and nurture are both critical to the individual, but other factors involving the inner person must be included as well—such as the thinking, feelings, beliefs and understanding of the individual and whatever attitudes, values and commitment a person may eventually acquire as a result of interrelationships which obtain among these factors. For example, a person could inherit a body type which tends to be either mesomorphic, ectomorphic or endomorphic, and with the introduction of proper diet and exercise we know that weight can be gained or lost, muscles toned, and endurance strengthened even though the individual's overall body type may remain within the same general classification. But whether or not an individual will embark on a program of improving personal health and fitness depends on a number of additional factors, not the least of which is how much importance and value the individual places on such activity. Admittedly, reinforcement does play a role. Many people have struggled to give up the more immediate personal pleasures of smoking or drinking to achieve the longer-term rewards associated with the improvement of personal health. But there also are people who will sacrifice these pleasures not so much because it is something which they really want to do, but because their family may have expressed concern about their health and it is something they believe they should do for the welfare of their family and to alleviate such worry.

In truth, learning, behavior and the realization of individual potential are not the exclusive result of either nature or nurture, or for that matter responses from the environment, but instead derive from a complex interaction among numerous factors including the characteristics and dispositions of the person; between whatever a person may be and possess in the way of attributes, values and beliefs, and the experiential environment with which he or she interacts. Consequently, whether or not behavior is shaped or determined in some fashion is not the issue, for it is determined; the issue concerns the complexity of behavior and the kinds of factors that can influence its direction and the form it assumes as it is played out existentially.

In Skinner's opinion, if we wish to change the behavior of a person, there is little point in considering the individual's reasoning, judgments, sense of responsibility, beliefs, values or feelings—the very things we believe are important characteristics of any person. True, we have conceded that reinforcement and our natural aversion to pain and punishment do represent powerful influences on behavior. And it also is true that when the lives of certain individuals are examined they seem to reveal a pattern of spontaneous reactions to events, with little or no reflection about why such events occur or how they might shape them or bring about some change in their direction. But missing in Skinner's environmental-human equation is the simple recognition that the relationship implied is more than reflexive and far more complex than he assumed. People are not simply acted upon, totally acquiescent and inert, to be pushed, shaped and molded like clay. The behaviorist assumes that our reactions are always beyond our choice and control, and this is where we disagree. If the values, thoughts and actions of others can become part of an environment which determines our behavior, why then cannot our own values, principles and reasoning have a similar role, that is, become factors which influence the course of our experience as well? We believe these factors can make a difference in the behavior of people;

that they influence the choices they make and accord a sufficient degree of personal autonomy to enable us to say that on many occasions people are responsible for what they do, despite the fact that operant-conditioning and prior environmental contingencies often are among these factors of influence. By virtue of reasoning and all that is involved in human cognition and emotion, the individual enters this equation representing an additional factor of influence. And it is because of this that many people do alter what they believe, do modify their opinions and thereby effect some change in their behavior and occasionally in the environment around them. It is precisely in the areas of human reasoning and reflection that we find personal autonomy and choice, and in the end responsibility.

The arguments outlined thus far point to our agreement with Gaylin that the variables potentially influencing our decisions and actions are seemingly infinite in number and are sufficiently varied in their nature and source to preclude the absolute predictability Skinner assumes, and to admit our personal intervention in the stream of events which make up the content and direction of our lives. Skinner fails to recognize what is unique about human beings, but the reality of human existence is treated superficially in other respects as well. In eliminating the concept of responsibility and the related notion of accountability, operant conditioning offers very little to go on if major social institutions are to make tough decisions and address the innumerable problems which arise as a matter of course in our everyday life.

> When a judge in a court of law is forced to distinguish between a free and a compelled act, he is not helped by being told by either a psychoanalyst or a behaviorist that all acts are compelled. Civilized society seems to require that there be a distinction between a man who violates the law with a gun pointed at his head and a man who commits the same violation for greed.[7]

Similarly, if a corporation is charged with dumping hazardous waste in an area in which it allegedly knew dumping was prohibited by law, and such an action has resulted in an unusual incidence of cancer or birth defects, a judge would not find it helpful to be told that the corporate officers who made the decision for this action were only doing what they had been conditioned to do and therefore were not responsible.

Responsibility in the field of education can involve legal conflicts and issues as well, issues which somehow must be resolved from the standpoint of determining responsibility and ultimately agent accountability. If a teacher draws the wrath of a community because she saw value in having her high school English class read *The Catcher in the Rye,* and if she is subsequently fired by the local school board, the court must somehow come to terms with the issue of parental and community rights versus the professional rights associated with academic freedom and the responsibility to promote what is in the best interest of the student. Inevitably, the court would have to resolve the issue by examining the respective actions and responsibilities of the teacher and the school board. The resolution of such an issue would be helped very little by saying that the teacher and the school board only did what they had been conditioned to do, even though a lifetime of conditioning influences may have played some part in influencing their respective perceptions and actions in the matter. The problems of personal and corporate accountability cannot be resolved by a deterministic theory of behavior which essentially contends that no one is really responsible for anything.

For these reasons, responsibility and the concept of accountability have validity. We take the position that people have some role in what they do, that however much their behavior and freedom may be conditioned by their environment and the vicissitudes of life, they nevertheless can reflect upon its events and attempt to come to terms with what it has to offer. Behaviorally, we may share some kinship with the animal host, but what is most distinctive about the evolution and development of the human species seems forgotten in Skinner's theory, and for this reason we find it wanting. In taking this position we are faced with the challenge of developing a concept of accountability which somehow reconciles the partial validity of Skinner's theory with our own belief that there are dimensions and a reality to behavior which it ignores. Skinner rejects the notion that people are responsible for what they do whether they act independently or collectively as members of a group; we have stated that personal and corporate responsibility is a primary element in justifying accountability obligations as well as the various requirements and relationships they impose. But other factors play an equally important role in establishing our accountability. As noted before, our lives involve a social as well as personal dimension; this social component is clearly evident not only in our relationships with other persons, but in the expectations associated with the various laws, moral beliefs and customs which are a part of the broader social structures to which we belong. Whether or not our actions and the roles we assume are believed to incur certain responsibilities and obligations is largely a function of these social institutions. It is for this reason that we now turn to the subject of moral and legal accountability. The moral and legal grounds for our obligations very much condition the nature of our accountability and have a direct bearing on the problem of agent compliance identified earlier. In the following chapter several distinctions will be drawn between moral and legal obligations, and two sets of factors will be identified which we believe have an influence on whether or not people are likely to honor their obligations once they have been established.

PART III

Agent compliance and the quality of accountability relationships

CHAPTER 5

Moral and legal accountability

We stated that obligations are defined by social custom and the moral and legal institutions of a society, and that people incur obligations because of their responsibility for acts, decisions or matters which involve the interests of others. The phrase *casual responsibility* was selected to identify explicit acts and decisions of an agent: murder, theft, willful trespass, saving a life, making and implementing policy decisions—these are only a few of the many types of actions that would have a prima facie classification within this category. But we also noted that people can acquire responsibilities in the form of expectations and performances that are associated with the various roles they might assume. Physicians and attorneys have certain responsibilities to their respective patients and clients which are expected of anyone who becomes a physician or an attorney and which are not generally expected of persons outside of these professions. Although several distinctions have been drawn between these categories of responsibility, in real-life situations they are often related. If the vice principal of a high school moves in to break up a fight between two students, by our analysis she would be casually responsible for her decisions and actions in dealing with the matter; but we also must recognize that she would be expected to take appropriate measures when confronted with a situation of this nature because it is she and not someone else who holds the position of vice principal, a position vested with supervisory authority and responsibilities she is expected to fulfill. Understandably, she may be called upon to justify the manner in which she handled this student confrontation, but because of the expectations associated with her professional role as an administrator she also could be called to account for failing to act or for ignoring the problem.

Agent freedom under moral and legal obligations

Many of the actions and matters for which people are responsible eventually become the basis for their obligations of accountability and to a considerable extent determine the various interpersonal and agency relationships they entail. When a person is expected to be accountable to others, we initially stated that the degree of accountability operating in such a relationship is a function of the expected form of accounting and the nature of the requirements it may impose. By our analysis the manner in which people are expected to be answerable is a factor influencing the degree of accountability operating on particular occasions and over a longer period within such relationships, but it is by no means the only factor. There may be justifiable grounds for saying that one person or group should be accountable to another, but it is one thing to justify an accountability obligation and quite a different matter to have assurance that some form of accounting will be provided. For this reason the degree of accountability that will exist in such relationships is very much conditioned by the element of agent compliance, that is, by whether or not the requirements of the obligation are likely to be satisfied.

The distinctions to be drawn between moral and legal accountability are important because they have a direct bearing on the problem of agent compliance. Suppose in our former example of a wife seeking a separation that a request for her reasons originates from a source in relation to which it is understood that she is *legally* obligated to respond, e.g., questions asked in court or through the exchange of interrogatories. Laws govern the procedures for terminating marriage because taking such a step is thought to be morally and socially significant. But while the law may be based on a recognition that in matters of this importance reasons *ought* to be given, law differs from morality in that it does not simply state what ought or ought not to be done in any given situation; rather, it stipulates what *is* or *is not* to be done under a given set of conditions. For example, would the identification of an obligation to account in either respect necessarily mean that accountability exists, in the sense that the wife would be "subject to" giving an account or that she would give it? These questions raise the problem of whether the notion of having an obligation to do something is entirely synonymous with being subject to doing it. There is reason to think not. If we inquire, "Is X accountable?" meaning "Is X obligated or subject to giving an account?" two interpretations are possible: We may be asking (1) whether under present circumstances there are any grounds to justify saying that X is obligated; or (2) to what extent X must satisfy the obligation, what latitude or discretion exists in having to satisfy it.

In the present case it has been determined that the wife could be morally or legally obligated to provide an account of her reasons; however, in regard to (2), under a moral obligation it seems incorrect to say that she is *subject to* giving it, for the question of its provision is largely a matter of whether she chooses to do so; in other words, it would depend largely on her recognition of the obligation. This would not be entirely the case where conditions of legal obligation obtain, for here the question of being subject to giving an account involves a number of factors extrinsic to her judgment; for example, whether the demand for an account originates from a source having the support of law and the degree to which she is free or unfree to refuse giving it under the law.

Of course, the former "moral obligation" is implied but under due process the court may ask for an account of the wife's reasons and do so on any number of occasions with the expectation that they will be given. So long as the relationship between the accounting agent and the party making the request has the support of law, in the absence of extenuating circumstances there appears to be a dimension to the obligation unlike that involved where moral obligations apply.

Several considerations must be distinguished in any circumstance of legal obligation: (1) the obligation itself, defined by the law specifying the conditions of its occurrence; (2) the amount of actual freedom or unfreedom attending the law—a function of its enforcement; (3) the degree to which an agent is *subject to* satisfying the obligation—a function of (2); and (4) whether the agent ultimately will or will not comply with what it requires.

For purposes of illustration, suppose that a law exists specifying a speed limit for a particular highway. With respect to (1), an agent would be legally obligated not to drive in excess of the speed limit. By legal definition he is formally unfree, that is, legally prohibited from doing so. Whether or not he will exceed the limit and comply with the law could depend on a number of factors: his physical/emotional state; driving conditions; his perception of the law's enforcement, i.e., his opinion concerning the probability that he may get caught should he choose to exceed it; and his attitude about one's obligation to obey the law. But the extent to which he is *subject to* satisfying (1) is a function of (2), enforcement of the law and the degree to which he is actually free or unfree to violate the speed limit under the due process and institution of law.

Two points are to be noted. First, the expectation of compliance does not vary with the degree of unfreedom attending a law. Normally, one is expected to comply because a legal obligation exists to do so, not because the law does or does not happen to be strictly enforced. For this reason it is important that a distinction be made between the formal compliance required by a legal obligation and the actual freedom one has to do or not to do whatever it enjoins. Probability of enforcement, in the present example, might include such factors as the number of patrol cars in relation to number of private vehicles on the highway; whether it is a general practice to issue tickets after apprehension and, if so, whether the system of due process is such that tickets must be paid. An individual's knowledge of these matters may extend only to a familiarity with how frequently the road is patrolled, or he may have good reason to believe that if he is caught it will be fairly easy to avoid the issuance of a ticket through discussion or bribery. For this reason enforcement of the law must be interpreted to include the system of due process and its quality. Since an agent's actual freedom is partly determined by considerations of this nature, we shall take the position that it is more correct to speak in terms of the *extent* to which an agent is subject to doing whatever a law requires, rather than in terms of his being either subject or not subject to doing it.

Second, to maintain that an agent is subject to the requirements of law to the extent that he is made unfree under it obviously means that where laws are seldom enforced this will be minimal; that his actual freedom or autonomy under these circumstances may be as great as his freedom under a moral obligation. But the foregoing is not generally presumed. Laws are brought into being for the purpose of assuring the fulfillment of obligations which society deems sufficiently important not to be left entirely to the moral attitude or personal discretion of its members. And it is in this respect that a different form of compliance is presupposed.

We must consider two counterarguments to this position because they introduce other factors which are important to the concept of accountability. Since public standards and various forms of social appraisal were stated to feature in our daily life, it could be argued that whether or not an individual or a group will satisfy a particular moral or legal obligation often depends on the influence of public opinion and the sanctions associated with prevailing attitudes. The distinction we are making does not deny that people frequently consult the opinion of others or seek some form of guidance or direction beyond themselves in making decisions; nor does it deny that some individuals will be guided almost entirely in their moral decisions by conventional standards and values. In another sense our moral freedom is even conditioned by our conscience and our loyalty to principles and values which we have chosen and believe are important. In moral situations of serious consequence, where acting on principle may require much of an individual, we understand the burden this freedom carries and the restriction on freedom the agent may feel. Nevertheless, law introduces still another dimension to the question of an agent's freedom which must be recognized. Conventional values and the opinion of reasonable men may very well indicate that an agent should give an account of something, e.g., disclosure of political campaign contributions. But in the absence of law, if he disavows the moral precepts underlying the obligation he could refuse for any number of reasons and be free to do so to the extent that the social opinion he challenges is unsupported by sanctions or nonlegal means of reprisal that would be significant to him. In essence, we do not deny that measures could be taken against him outside of the law and that this would be a factor conditioning his freedom, but laws have the feature of applying to all parties defined by the conditions of their application; whether persons happen to base their moral decisions on whim, public opinion or a personal theory of moral obligation is incidental to the fact that, theoretically, they would be formally obligated by what a given law specifies and actually subject to what it requires to the extent of its enforcement.

The second argument would maintain that this is precisely the point. In similar circumstances individuals may be equally bound by the law theoretically, but whether they will actually comply is still largely a matter of personal choice, not enforcement, as evidenced by the fact that some individuals either disavow laws, ignore their requirements or choose to protest what a given law may require on the grounds that it seriously conflicts with moral principles to which they assign a greater moral priority. The fact that some individuals have little regard for law and weigh the probabilities of legal enforcement in making a decision to comply, or that others may engage in acts of civil disobedience on the basis of moral principle, is not being questioned; what is being questioned is the degree of independence presumed and the assumption that their *overall* freedom to disobey the law is similar to that associated with situations of strictly moral obligation.

The basic problem here centers on the apparent antinomy between an individual's freedom of choice under either form of obligation, which I think we must admit does exist, and our saying that when a legal obligation is present an agent is actually unfree to violate it to the extent of its enforcement. This is well illustrated by the example of Martin Luther King during the civil rights movement. King engaged in acts of civil disobedience on the grounds that unjust laws occasionally come into being, laws which degrade the human spirit to such an extent that common decency and a sense of justice require one not to obey them. In following this belief King was arrested and placed in jail. There he drafted a letter explaining that we are obligated to obey laws which are just and designed to improve the human condition, yet equally obligated to resist those which are unjust, especially when normal channels of recourse are closed.

The circumstances under which this letter was written attest to King's freedom of moral choice even when faced with a legal obligation to the contrary. It is important that an individual's freedom in this respect be recognized, as well as the fact that it generally prevails even under conditions of legal obligation; but we also must recognize that the letter was written in jail, and though King's moral freedom existed there, his personal freedom was not without constraint. He could not under these conditions be with his family, travel or pursue certain civil rights activities. While compelling reasons supported his moral refusal to obey the law, he was nevertheless subject to it.

Though people honor or fail to honor obligations for a variety of reasons and acts of civil disobedience may sometimes be morally justified, it is assumed that legal institutions exist to make explicit what various groups within a society value, and because not all persons are motivated to fulfill the obligations which reasonable people acknowledge. Where moral argument or sensitivity have failed to persuade some individuals to a course of action believed to be right and fitting or to dissuade them from the opposite, legal requirements often have, and the fact that for some they have not simply indicates that people will vary in their response to the moral and legal obligations they incur.

While identification of either form of obligation is not a sufficient condition for saying that an agent will give an account or that he will be subject to doing so, our initial position is that moral and legal obligations involve this difference. Under circumstances in which it is justifiable to maintain that X is *morally accountable* to Y, and both a legal obligation and extralegal means of coercion are absent, we may only go so far as to say that X is morally obligated to give an account, not that X is "subject to" doing so. Admittedly, if the reasons underlying the obligation are morally compelling and the agent is a morally sensitive person, probability of compliance may be very high, and it could be high if he is subject to threat or other forms of pressure. But where it is justifiable to maintain that X is *legally accountable* to Y, we can interpret this to mean that X is legally obligated to give an account *and* is "subject to" doing so to the extent that he is actually unfree to do otherwise under the legal authority defining his relationship to Y. An agent in this latter instance may be morally motivated to comply, but if he is not, he must still contend with the implications of due process and whatever its associated procedures may circumstantially involve.

It is our position that legal obligations introduce an additional compliance factor in the manner stated, but if accountability relationships do occasionally require the moral formal status offered by law, there is the problem of what differences are to be drawn between the institution of law, which appears to be an institution of accountability, on the one hand, and on the other hand extralegal relationships of accountability which exist as a matter of course in our lives. It is quite possible that a concept of accountability can become meaningless and convey little of a distinctive sort if it is too broadly interpreted or too closely identified with legal procedure. Is there a point demarcating what this concept may be reasonably said to comprehend and what is normally expected under the due process of law? Though this question is difficult and will remain open to argument, a tentative position is offered.

Difficulties with the relationship between law and accountability are partly due to the fact that certain features of each are necessary to the other. It has been stated that implicit in the notion of being "subject to" is the element of unfreedom to do otherwise; that this element may legitimately obtain under the constraints imposed by law or an authority having its support; and that the more formal status of law is sometimes crucial to the difference between having someone's obligation to give an account and having some assurance that it will be given. On the other hand, various forms of accounting such as relating, describing, explaining, and justifying feature importantly in judicial procedure as do other, more stringent forms of being answerable. What must be distinguished, then, is the institution of law, in which certain elements of accountability play an important part and to which those who are affected by what it enjoins may be accountable, and a relationship of accountability which may or may not have the support of law but which may be justifiable on other grounds.

Laws instituted to establish an initial accountability relationship among parties within society are to be distinguished from those laws whose primary intention is to establish an immediate accountability to law and the agencies of its enforcement. Laws prohibiting murder, theft, motor vehicle violations, and pollution of water or air, represent the latter; laws which require public disclosure of ingredients on packaging, the source and amounts of campaign contributions, or statements of financial condition, or which establish direct grievance procedures between producer and consumer, exemplify the former. The creation of any law immediately establishes an actual accountability to the extent of its enforcement, but it is important to distinguish instances in which one's accountability is directly to the law from those in which this is but a potential condition supporting some form of interagent relationship.[1]

The presumption in favor of moral accountability

A further issue is relevant to the relationship between moral and legal accountability. We have stated that the element of agent compliance is an important consideration in accountability relationships. From a moral point of view it may be reasonable to expect candidates to account for their financial affairs over the course of a political campaign. But if they repeatedly fail to reveal the identity of sources which contribute to their financial base and represent a potential source of influence and control, one may well question how much accountability really exists. Although a fairly high or low degree of accountability is possible in both moral and legal relationships, it is understandable that laws have been enacted to provide greater assurance of financial disclosure.

However, when and according to what considerations a moral obligation to account should be assigned the status of a legal obligation is an important issue. Several points brought out in the discussion thus far weigh in favor of legal accountability. First, as noted earlier, men are motivated differently in their response to the obligations they incur. But though some are persistent in their attempts to circumvent the law, even when the risks are high, it is assumed that for the majority this is generally untrue; that among the latter are many who recognize the need for law, the general obligation to obey it on logical and ethical grounds, as well as those who do so mainly because of their orientation to conventional opinion or through fear of the reprisals and stigma which attend its violation. Why not, then, give legal status to any accountability relationship, thereby introducing the additional motivation and compliance factor which certain individuals require? In essence, this argument contends that the morally conscientious will probably honor reasonable obligations to account anyway, so why not extend the efficacy of such relationships by providing an inducement for those not so inclined, who respond appropriately only when faced with the authority of law?

There also is the argument that law serves an additional function beyond that of compliance. Where conflicts of interest arise and the respective claims of individuals are complicated, laws provide a public and supposedly impartial standard to which all might appeal for their adjudication, and there is little reason to assume that relationships of accountability would be any less complicated, as suggested by many examples in the areas of presidential accountability and consumer affairs. Therefore, would it not be desirable to incorporate the rather definitive guidelines which laws provide in arrangements of this nature?

Admittedly, even where a rational form of existence is preferred there is little reason to suppose that it would preclude need for the procedural and compliance characteristics of law either generally or in certain of the accountability relationships occurring within it. People simply do not arrive in life fully developed as moral beings, and history provides ample evidence that a disturbing number never reach this state. But the foregoing only points to the fact that the law exists not as an end in itself, but as a sometimes necessary expedient for bringing about what is thought to be. The real issue here is not the necessity for law, which must be granted, but what any law fully implies when it is brought into being and how this implication coheres with other features of the life it is designed to promote. If freedom is a necessary and important feature in societies structured around principles of democracy and rational procedure, then any move to restrict it should be approached with caution and occur only when there are good reasons for doing so. Law represents such a move, for it can only fulfill its compliance and procedural functions at the expense of freedom, upon which the constraints it imposes necessarily infringe. Obviously, these grounds will exist, as would be true when the exercise of freedom on the part of one individual unjustifiably restricts that of another or poses some manner of injury that ought to be prevented. Some have argued, and quite effectively, that the very freedom we wish to defend can only exist if a people are willing to accept a system of constraints by which it can be assured—e.g., laws designed to guarantee freedom of speech, worship, assembly, petition, the right of ownership, and so forth—but which do so only by making each of us legally unfree to interfere with others where these things are at issue.[2]

But again, what this confirms is the occasional need for law as a means of promoting what is believed to be of value, and relevant grounds have certainly existed to justify legal pronouncements in these areas. The point we wish to make is that a presumption in favor of freedom requires that more be considered in the notion of "relevant grounds" for imposing a constraint than merely identifying a class of acts as being sufficiently important to warrant some form of social concern. What should be demonstrated from the standpoint of freedom is that other, less restrictive approaches to preventing an undesirable act are either unavailable or ineffectual.

Consider the apparently simple case of leaving a key in the ignition of an unattended automobile. The act itself is innocent enough, and one would presume a right to do it under the commonly accepted notion of ownership. But it has been demonstrated that however innocent it may be, the act of leaving a key in an unattended car establishes more favorable conditions for theft to occur. The latter is clearly injurious to the public interest. The loss in real value each year runs into the millions and is often reflected in higher insurance rates, even for many who never follow this practice. Expense to the public is also brought about by the attention which law enforcement officials must give to arrest, prosecution, imprisonment or monitoring probation once a theft has been reported—a cost in time and money which could be devoted to other matters. The injury involved in cases of auto theft may be even more direct since auto theft sometimes ends in high-speed pursuit and accidents which injure not only the delinquent but police and innocent parties as well.

Understandably, whether or not something should be done to prevent people from leaving keys in their cars would depend on the extent to which this act is a contributory factor in auto theft. Although there is evidence that it is, according to our position, before a law is put into effect making a considerable number of people formally and actually unfree to commit an act, which occurs frequently in a normal course of events, alternative means of discouraging the act should be explored, e.g., providing information about the seriousness of the problem through advertising and licensing procedure, or installing devices which warn a driver when keys have been left—methods that are now being tried. The advantage of such procedures is that one might achieve the desired result by appealing to the reason and judgment of people, leaving the decision with them rather than limiting their freedom categorically. Of course, if these alternatives prove ineffective and the problem continues, a prohibitory law may be required.

Now some may concede the above, but rejoin that the argument given thus far makes it possible to interpret law, freedom and even accountability as simply different means by which more valued ends are achieved. And if this is the case, then where it is essential that an agent be accountable to satisfy some higher purpose, it really makes little difference how much freedom is claimed as long as the necessary accountability is attained. One is merely substituting one means for another. Stated as it is, the preceding criticism has a point. Any accountability relationship is no better than the likelihood of an agent's compliance with what it requires, and occasionally the additional compliance factor provided under a legal obligation may be necessary.

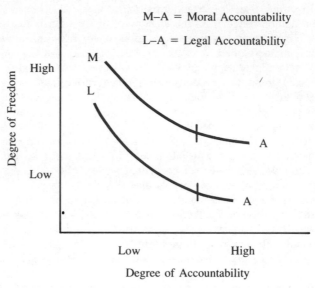

Fig. 5.1

The curve *LA* in figure 5.1 presents the relationship existing among the factors of legal constraint, accountability and freedom under the preceding interpretation. It suggests that their relationship is essentially indifferent at any point on the curve, since a loss in freedom due to legal constraint is compensated by a greater degree of accountability, and that when accountability becomes less important and the compliance associated with it diminishes, a greater degree of freedom occurs. But how much freedom would supporters of this argument be willing to sacrifice to bring about a particular degree of accountability?

Perhaps the relationship between freedom and accountability is indifferent when the legal accountability established is justified and of primary importance, but a further difference between moral and legal obligations must be observed. The former obligate us to do something only when there are ethical considerations, such as moral principles and values to support them. It would be a logical absurdity to assert that one is morally obligated to do something, but that his obligation lacks moral justification or that the performance to which it commits him is morally reprehensible. Moral obligations can only exist if they are defensible on moral grounds, but the same is not true for all legal obligations. To be sure, legal obligations which seem justifiable usually rest on ethical considerations which are logically prior and to which we ultimately appeal for their justification, e.g., that this law should exist because it is in the common interest, protects individual rights or promotes what is thought to be of value. But it is possible to create laws devoid of any moral justification, or for that matter laws that are highly undesirable from a moral point of view. Laws have existed which arbitrarily discriminated in favor of a select few or threatened individual life and property, as was true under the Nuremburg edicts in the mid-thirties, and certain laws of the United States have been unjustifiably discriminatory from a moral point of view, promoting inequality of opportunity and the denial of basic rights. Nevertheless, they obligate one legally, if not morally, when they originate from a central authority having power to enact and enforce them. Our position is that where laws are capricious, arbitrary or unjust, the degree of freedom lost in the name of whatever purpose they serve is not a matter of indifference and that this would be equally true where accountability is involved. Figure 5.1 demonstrates the point made earlier concerning moral accountability and what it implies about the overall freedom of an agent. When the degree of accountability is high, under a moral obligation one would assume that it is because of the agent's sensitivity to the moral reasons or conventional attitudes supporting the obligation. True, he may feel constrained, feel that his freedom is much less than it would be if these reasons and attitudes did not exist. But again, the constraint he feels is largely a matter of *his* perception of the obligation and its validity; it is not due to the external and probable intervention in his life that a legal obligation represents. While the degree of accountability achieved under either form of obligation may be high on many occasions, an agent's autonomy and overall freedom are more extensive under moral accountability; this is suggested by the relative position of the *MA* curve in figure 5.1.

However, alternatives to law which rely on the judgment, reason and morality of a people are to be preferred not only because they are less restrictive of freedom, but because they are more consistent with the ideal features presupposed by a rational way of living and what is expected of those who are a part of it. There is a sense in which the need for laws represents a falling short of this ideal. When laws must be enacted guaranteeing a minority group rights or opportunities which as a matter of course are assumed by a majority, such laws not only signify the importance of these things to any individual's pursuit of a decent life, but attest to the lack of moral sensitivity and practice on the part of those who make such laws necessary. Our position, then, does not deny the need for law or legal accountability, for it is obvious that some people are unreasonable or are morally insensitive to concerns which involve the rights and interests of others; it simply holds that if there are several ways to accomplish a justifiable end, all else being equal, those which are less restrictive of freedom are preferable for the reasons stated.

Agent compliance and moral outlook

The preceding analysis attempts to accommodate and work out various aspects of freedom which attend obligations of a moral and legal sort, and introduces initial factors which have a bearing on the problem of agent compliance.[3] But though we must grant the additional compliance motivation that laws can provide because of their associated enforcement, our analysis has introduced nonlegal influences on an individual which are extremely important to the concept of accountability. Even the problem of legal compliance is complicated by the fact that people differ in their view of the law, in how they perceive their responsibilities and obligations, and most assuredly in the kinds of considerations that are likely to influence their actions. As noted, some individuals will run extreme risks to achieve personal gain by violating laws that are strictly enforced, while others take a more cautious view in estimating a law's enforcement and whether they think they can "get by" with breaking it. In contrast, there are other people who have a strong "law and order" orientation. In their opinion laws should be obeyed regardless of what they require simply because they are the law. Ironically, while such persons may be law abiding, an unquestioned obedience to law can result in practices and a system of social compliance which are just as injurious in their effects as those resulting from criminal actions. The Nuremburg edicts mentioned earlier evolved from discriminatory laws and practices that had existed in Germany for many years, and we observed that under the authority of law several states followed discriminatory practices in relation to a black minority that the responsible majority would never have wanted to endure.

There are individuals who appear to be devoid of any personal autonomy in their moral life and whose actions seem to be guided almost exclusively by the dictates of authority or by how others will react to what they do. Coupled with a strong need for approval, the collective behavior of such persons can lead to an unquestioning loyalty which is formed around the expectations of the individuals or groups dominating their allegiance. The fact that extreme conformity can be demanded of persons belonging to particular subgroups of society is well illustrated by the conformity expected of individuals who are members of certain motorcycle gangs or teenage peer groups, even though both may go to great lengths in demonstrating their noncomformity with society and its values. In making these observations we are not denying the necessity for groups to have expectations of their members or the fact that groups are indispensable if society is to function. Much like society in general, the welfare of groups can only be secured through a general acceptance of the rules and values by which their essential character is defined and their particular functions are promoted. Nevertheless, it seems clear from what happened in Nazi Germany and from other examples we have given that the way in which people are morally oriented to what others expect is an important issue. Group associations are necessary, but it is equally true that they are by no means uniformly commendable in the ideals and activities they pursue. Organized crime and the Ku Klux Klan are not the only organizations that have pursued a collective self-interest at the expense of the welfare, rights and sometimes the lives of other persons. In a very real sense they survive as organizations and are able to engage in such activities because their members are indifferent to their complicity in actions which inflict on others what they would not wish to have inflicted on themselves.

Fortunately, people differ in their view of life. Whether or not some individuals will conform to the expectations of others or honor particular obligations depends on a range of considerations that are more comprehensive than simply "What will they think?", "Where will this get me?" or "That's the law and that's all there is to it." Among these considerations will be those which are relevant to the particular occasion of the obligation, e.g., whether the associated expectations and requirements are fair, morally sound or can be met under the circumstances, or whether there are special considerations to warrant modifying what is expected. Beyond these circumstantial considerations, of which there could be any number, there are other factors of a more general sort which serve as the means by which individuals assess moral situations and the expectations that others may have. These factors would include the moral orientation, values and beliefs of the individual, how the individual reasons and the degree of independence and personal autonomy the individual generally brings to situations in which he or she must deal with normative matters. There are people who recognize the importance of law, the need for loyalty and social values, but who also realize that they have a personal responsibility where moral issues and human expectations are concerned. The degree to which laws are enforced may sometimes influence what they do, but generally their compliance derives from a recognition that laws are necessary to ensure the welfare of society and to secure the rights and interests of other persons as well as their own. We believe that morally sensitive individuals who possess a degree of personal autonomy and the disposition to think for themselves, although similar to our "law and order" person in being generally law abiding, are more likely to question the expectations of others. And we believe they are less inclined to accept the position that authority, tradition or the dictates of any particular group are sufficient in themselves to justify what may be morally right or wrong. Research has established that individuals differ in how they approach and reason about ethical problems and that some people have a broader perspective regarding the considerations that may be relevant to any given moral issue.

When an individual is consistent in meeting obligations which appear reasonable, and he or she is noted for doing so, we generally say that the person has a strong "sense of obligation." In customary usage this phrase is intended to convey a general impression about a person's character based on various observations of the individual's behavior. The character and typical behavior of people are factors quite relevant to the problem of agent compliance, but for our purpose it will be helpful to distinguish between the longer-term behavior associated with an individual and the probability that he or she will comply with any given obligation in a particular set of circumstances. Although we know that there are people who have a strong sense of obligation, it does not follow from this fact about their character that they will always satisfy the obligations they are alleged to have. The probability of their compliance in any given situation will depend on the interaction and degree of influence that exist among the circumstantial, personal and social factors we have mentioned and in the end obtain as a result of the individual's general sense of obligation. Whether the person is essentially moral or amoral, guided primarily by a personal code of ethics or by the opinions and expectations of others, in using this phrase we really imply the following: All things considered, what is the person's attitude toward the obligation, and given the individual's sense of it, is the obligation something with which the individual is likely to comply? In essence, the degree to which people will honor their obligations ultimately is a function of how they interpret them and the kinds of considerations that are most likely to motivate their compliance or noncompliance. For the sake of discussion we shall group these factors into two general categories of influence.

I. The moral orientation of the individual or group.
    Here we include the predominant values and beliefs of the individual or group, the moral principles to which they subscribe, their general performance in relation to their obligations and responsibilities, the manner in which they view the expectations, rights and interests of others, the level of their moral development and the sophistication with which they approach and reason about ethical problems.
II. The circumstantial considerations attending the obligation.
    A. For example, whether the obligation is reasonable and fair in what it requires.
        1. From the standpoint of accountability, is the obligation justifiable under the circumstances? That is, has the agent's casual or expectational responsibility been demonstrated in relation to the matters for which the agent is expected to be answerable, and do those expecting some form of accounting have a valid interest and entitlement in such matters?
        2. Under the circumstances, it is possible for the individual or group to meet the requirements imposed by the expected form of accounting, and is it possible to satisfy the expectations associated with the relationship it involves?

3. How compatible is fulfillment of the obligation with other obligations of the agent that may have equal or greater validity?
B. To what degree is the agent "subject to" complying by means of legal enforcement, possible retribution or coercion?

The circumstantial considerations identified above are relevant to obligations of accountability, but for other kinds of obligations they will vary depending on the nature of the situation. People usually encounter situations in which both categories of influence come into play and together affect their decisions and subsequent actions. The circumstances of life can pose serious ethical questions which challenge the values and moral beliefs of the individuals involved and call upon whatever moral orientation they may have in coming to terms with the practical and normative issues they face. For example, within a corporation run autocratically, the decision to get rid of hazardous waste by knowingly dumping it in an area where dumping is prohibited by law could very well be unilateral and implemented on the authority of one individual; but in other circumstances a decision of this nature could result from the majority vote or consensus of a group of individuals and be carried out on the basis of the collective power of their positions despite legal prohibitions. In deliberating about such a decision, each individual brings to the situation his or her own values, beliefs, particular way of reasoning and moral point of view, however commendable or questionable they may be, and each must deal with a number of circumstantial factors of common concern as well as considerations that may be relevant only to the particular interests of certain individuals. In the present example these considerations might include the fact that the company is in serious financial trouble and faces the reality that legitimate means of disposal involve exorbitant costs, while the failure to carry them out involves the possibility of adverse publicity and having to pay severe penalties. These considerations have to be weighed against the fact that the proposed method of disposal is not only illegal but poses a serious threat to the health and perhaps even the lives of people who live near the selected disposal site. Faced with a serious fiscal crisis, the knowledge that stockholders have grown increasingly discontented over the financial health of the company and that he or a number of his employees may lose their jobs, the company president may decide to take a risk and go along with the recommendation, arguing that he must protect the welfare of his employees and the interests of his stockholders. On the other hand, he may decide to veto the proposal, believing that the danger it presents to others is an overriding consideration and that, if carried out, the group's recommendation would be unacceptable morally as well as legally. Furthermore, it is possible that the president could make this decision knowing full well that the other problems will still exist, however difficult and unsolvable they may seem at the time.

Others within the group might struggle with these same concerns or care little about the danger to other people which the recommendation involves, believing that the welfare of the company and its survival are the only issues.

Individual considerations could be involved as well: By virtue of their office, the president and other high-ranking officials may be secure in voicing their opinions, while a junior executive may know that despite the grounds supporting his position, to voice it strongly on the basis of his moral convictions could very well result in his being transferred or fired. In real-life situations individuals and groups are often confronted with problems involving moral and practical considerations similar to the above. Finding a solution to such problems and making the difficult choices they require can test our abilities and the courage to stand by our convictions. Taking a moral stand may be fairly easy when it has the general support of a group, but if it is unpopular, the personal price for taking it can be considerable, to say the least.

In maintaining that the moral orientation of a group and its members has a lot to do with how they view ethical issues and ultimately address moral and legal obligations, we are really saying two things which at first may seem to be in contradiction, but actually are not. First, from the standpoint of insight and substance, the deliberations of the group will be no better than whatever its individual members bring to them, and the outcome of such deliberations is a function of the relative influence which individual opinions have upon the group as a whole. But group processes are complex from a psychological and political standpoint; they can be carried out democratically in a climate which encourages the expression of differing points of view or conducted in an atmosphere dominated by a power hierarchy whose agenda or security will allow only those views it wishes to hear. Reasonable people might agree with our junior executive that he is morally correct in objecting to the recommended manner for disposing of this waste, but he and other members of the group may be overruled for a variety of reasons, with the outcome that a company policy is implemented on the basis of a group decision that is quite contrary to the beliefs of its dissenting members. Consequently, our second point is simply this: that however important the moral orientation and contributions of individual members are to the process of reaching a decision, ultimately the group will have a collective moral character of its own. The group's final decision and the actions that are subsequently promoted will say a great deal about the group as a whole as well as the company it represents.

Eventually this company may be held accountable for illegal waste disposal. If we are correct in arguing that individual or corporate responsibility is a primary element in establishing and attributing obligations of accountability, then in such an event ethical considerations would continue to apply. As noted before, many of the expectational responsibilities associated with the roles people acquire evolve from an underlying code of values that are presupposed even where responsibilities are assigned by the formal dictates of law or on the basis of rule or policy within the organizational structures to which they belong. Much the same can be said about responsibilities of a casual sort, for it is largely on the basis of moral precepts, accepted values, social custom and the law that the content of our actions and treatment of others are judged to be acceptable or unacceptable and, as we stated before, that we distinguish between behavior for which we ought to be accountable and behavior that is really a matter of our own business.

Once again, the preceding illustrates the point that there is a social as well as a personal dimension to morality. Our moral beliefs and actions are not matters which are entirely individual, for they are often measured in relation to the standards and values which prevail in the cultures where they occur. The institution of law is a social contrivance designed to formalize and provide publicity for the values and rules by which a society elects to regulate its affairs. The moral positions assumed by society, its institutions and groups create expectations with respect to our actions and the roles we occupy. Accordingly, they condition our actions, and whether or not we choose, through ignorance, indifference or moral beliefs, to follow a course that runs counter to them does not alter the reality of the consequences that can attend our actions because they exist. Thus, the way in which we view and are morally oriented to such expectations is an important factor in establishing our accountability to others as well as the form it is likely to assume. Skinner may reject the concept of responsibility, but in reality our accountability is very much a function of the manner in which we treat the expectations associated with these broader social institutions.

At the same time, the relationship between a society and its members is by no means one-sided and in reality is mutually conditioning. The welfare and direction of any society are very much influenced by the moral orientation of its members. Although laws exist prohibiting murder, violent assault, rape and theft, these crimes are committed every day and attest to the fact that the legal and moral threads that bind the fabric of society are perhaps more fragile than many realize. Whether such crimes are premeditated or committed out of passion, it is clear that those who commit them have little recognition or regard for the rights and interests of others. And yet it is neither possible nor desirable to have a law enforcement officer on every street corner. If we are to avoid the conditions of a police state, then to remain viable the institution of law must rely on more than strict enforcement. As a primary social institution it must depend upon a general recognition of the importance of laws and the values, principles and rights they attempt to secure. Where laws are just and reasonable, legal institutions must assume that people will recognize their justification and will comply with what they require out of a sense of responsibility and obligation. Thus, the additional compliance factors associated with the law do have a bearing on the degree to which a person will be "subject to" giving an account, but as we have stated before, whether or not an agent will honor a moral or a legal obligation of accountability ultimately depends on the same complex of factors that govern his recognition and fulfillment of other obligations.

Earlier the position was taken that laws are a formal articulation of what a society or particular groups believe to be important, and that they presuppose an underlying moral code and ethical principles. We also noted that for a society to endure its practices must reflect fidelity to the fundamental principles upon which it is structured. For this reason, when legislators pass and impose arbitrary and unjust laws, and when law enforcement officials violate the law or the rights of people in carrying out their work, they sow the seeds of disrespect and may be as responsible for undermining the institution of law as others who flagrantly disregard it.

Our example concerning a corporate decision to dispose of hazardous waste suggests that the quality of life and the welfare of people can be greatly affected by decisions and actions which are taken on the basis of the moral outlook of persons other than themselves, whether the former act independently or collectively as a group. It is in view of this that we now turn to the subject of student accountability. Maturational processes inevitably project youth into an adult world whether they are adequately prepared or are ready emotionally or psychologically for the responsibilities commonly expected of adults. To say that today's youth are tomorrow's adults and that our youth are the promise of the future are clichés, but true nevertheless. Whether the choice is one of taking drugs or disposing of hazardous waste, in their present life and in the various roles or positions they will eventually assume, students must face moral problems and make difficult moral choices as serious as the examples we have given in this and preceding chapters. How they address the challenges before them will depend to a considerable extent on their values and moral outlook. In the next chapter we shall focus on the moral development of youth and the manner in which we believe their accountability ought to be approached, particularly where their behavior and learning are concerned. In the process of examining issues relating to the accountability of students, additional positions will be taken which have implications for accountability relationships in general.

CHAPTER 6

The accountability and moral development of students

Student responsibility and contemporary culture

In the literature which deals with accountability in education the subject of student accountability is seldom mentioned. Nevertheless, several considerations justify treating it as a specific subject. First, the various forms of accounting described earlier were stated to be a central element in accountability relationships, indispensable to effective communication, and as such they represent skills which must be developed and included among the primary aims of education. Second, the groundwork for our moral development is established during the formative years of our youth and for most children while they are in school and under the influence of adult supervision. As more indeterminate dispositions, the sense of responsibility and the moral awareness we hope to instill in children must be developed over a long period of time and by their nature require that we initiate this development during these early years of dependence. We indicated that some parents operate on this assumption and that throughout these years by example, discussion, assigning responsibilities and holding their children answerable they strive to influence the development of these dispositions and the attitudes upon which they depend.

Presumably, the passage from childhood through adolescence and into adulthood is a period of growth and maturing; few would debate the fact that these years are formative, and because of this the concept of accountability and its role in education require a broader interpretation. Through the programs and curricula they promote, the activities and aims they pursue, and the atmosphere they maintain, schools influence the values and moral beliefs of their students, the way in which students view rules and authority. We believe they have the potential to affect the sense of obligation and responsibility students ought to acquire. Schools are by no means an exclusive factor in these matters, for their influence, like that of parents, is very much conditioned by other factors; however, four things are being assumed at this point: (1) that whether or not people recognize the rights of others and honor their obligations is very much a function of their values and moral orientation; (2) that the moral orientation and values of people are significantly influenced by the learning and experiences of their youth; (3) that by virtue of the number of years children are in school, schools have a role to play in furthering their moral development, despite the fact that other factors may be as crucial from the standpoint of influencing such development; and (4) that, much like adults, the way in which students handle their responsibilities and obligations will very much determine the nature of their accountability while they are students and when they assume the responsibilities associated with being adults.

But there is another reason for turning to the subject of student accountability. Students may not have the degree of responsibility[1] normally associated with being an adult, but they too have responsibilities for which they must be accountable. While they are in school they must answer for their behavior and for what they are expected to learn, and where the rights and interests of others are concerned, the institutional contexts and structures for their accountability will vary depending on whether the matters in question involve the home, friends, employers, the law, various government agencies or other persons in the community. Seemingly, the circumstances of our accountability can be as varied as the activities and interpersonal relationships which characterize our lives, and in this respect students are similar to adults.

At the same time, a number of considerations complicate the subject of student accountability. One of the first difficulties is the special status that students have during their pre-adult years. Though we know that maturity is not automatically given to people at a certain age and that some children are more mature at thirteen than some adults ever will be, our society assumes that there is a time for childhood and "growing up." Children make mistakes and often fail to do what is right or expected, but because of their age and inexperience we generally modify our expectations of them and the responsibilities we believe it is appropriate for them to have, even though we know that requiring them to answer for their behavior is an important factor in furthering their development. Children must be held accountable for certain casual and expectational responsibilities, but our culture also recognizes the typical immaturity of their age and it is generally assumed that their accountability before the law and within the home and the school should be approached with this recognition in mind. Though increasingly challenged, it is a common assumption that juveniles who break the law or commit criminal offenses should be treated differently than adult offenders. Adults also make mistakes, but because of their expected maturity by virtue of being adults we tend to believe that they should be more responsible, and as a consequence their actions can result in more stringent forms of accountability.

A second problem encountered in approaching the question of student accountability relates to the social and cultural milieu in which children must develop today. From the standpoint of individual cases, one cannot demonstrate that growing up in the 1980s is more difficult than growing up in earlier times, for there will always be examples of hardship from the past that on reflection would seem insurmountable even by today's experience. Trying to survive in a new country, making adjustments to its language, customs and unfortunately too often to its prejudices undoubtedly imposed hardship on scores of immigrant parents and their children, and there are many adults who remember quite vividly what it was like to grow up during the Depression. But despite the struggles with economic deprivation and cultural adjustment which earlier generations had to endure, it was possible for children in rural and even urban America to grow up under the influence of a more circumscribed set of beliefs and values. For the most part the dominant values were those espoused by their parents, the school and the church, and those closely associated with their neighborhood and ethnic culture. These influences continue, but they no longer go unchallenged. Parents who strive to instill particular values or a sense of responsibility in their children must do so in competition with powerful influences. The technological advances in mass communication over the past fifty years have benefited this nation considerably, but these same advances also mean that values and beliefs can no longer be isolated. Daily, the youth of this nation are confronted with extensive amounts of information containing innumerable ideas, values and beliefs, much of which is confusing, in mutual conflict and certainly no longer confined to those things that either the school or their parents may favor.

The examples are obvious but nevertheless important. We have structured our entertainment and sell clothing, tonic, cars and other media products largely on the focus of sex, youth and the goals of success and material well-being. Whether it is the television programing they watch, the magazines they read or the music they listen to, children are constantly reminded that despite adult pronouncements these things must be important for they are emphasized everywhere. Yet when youth have questions about their sexuality or seek assistance in dealing with the problems that may be a consequence of their sexual activity, many people recoil in horror at the thought that schools or other community agencies should have programs to deal with these issues. In a similar vein, adults often tell children that honesty is the best policy and try to teach nonviolence, but our sporting events, films, books and television programs depict a great deal of violence and, in reporting the news, print and television media frequently reveal that there are many adults who do believe that crime pays. The incidence of alcoholism and drug abuse among the young is serious and should not be ignored, but conscientious adults concerned about these problems are faced with trying to do something about them in a society where the use of drugs has become more prevalent in business, sports and a number of prestigious professions. These problems are serious enough in themselves but they also complicate the issue of student accountability. How can we promote the ideals that students ought to be sensitive to the rights of others, have a sense of responsibility and obligation, and pursue goals in life that are worthwhile and consistent with what is legally and morally right when they have so many examples to the contrary. Some individuals will assign a different level of importance to these problems and disagree with our position that they present a significant challenge to the welfare of this nation and its youth, but this does not change the fact that today students must somehow develop an identity and arrive at a conception of what they ought to be as adults within a culture that often presents them with double standards and a serious conflict in values. The basic question is how the accountability and moral development of youth should be approached given the issues we have identified and the contemporary culture in which both must be addressed. The research of Lawrence Kohlberg provides at least a partial and we believe important answer to this question.

Kohlberg's theory of cognitive-moral development

In discussing the "hidden curriculum," Kohlberg emphasized that actions often speak louder than words, and he stressed the influence that adult behavior and modeling can have upon the young, particularly during periods in their development when they strive to emulate adult behavior. But the value of Kohlberg's research reaches far beyond this observation. His studies focus on cognitive-moral development and on strategies that are effective in promoting the moral development and insight of children and adults. These studies reveal more than we have discussed to this point about the reasoning and considerations that determine how people interpret human actions and responsibility in moral situations and why they believe certain actions to be morally right or wrong. Kohlberg identifies several factors which he and his colleagues believe are paramount in the moral development and outlook of people. These same factors closely parallel several of the elements which we have argued are central to the concept of accountability. Although the focus of Kohlberg's research does not support a theory sufficiently comprehensive to account for all aspects of human behavior (nor does it purport to do so) and a comprehensive analysis of it is clearly beyond the scope of this study, it must be examined because of its relevance to the issues we have raised. We shall find that Kohlberg's research does not preclude the influence and value of operant conditioning, but if Kohlberg is correct, Skinner's theory must be viewed in a different light.

Generally speaking, when people are confronted with the circumstances of a moral problem, they have conceptions of what ought or ought not to be done, a point of view about which actions are right or wrong and should or should not be taken in such situations. We agree with R. M. Hare that serious moral issues ought to be approached as rationally and objectively as possible, but this does not mean that these elements are clearly evident in the behavior of people on all occasions or imply that everyone reasons well. The judgments of people often reflect shallow or faulty reasoning, and show little awareness of the circumstantial considerations relevant to the moral issues or problems with which they are involved; and, from the standpoint of moral beliefs and values, the behavior or some people will reflect a moral posture that is exclusively self-interested or devoid of any sensitivity to moral principle. But the fact that certain individuals behave in this manner does not change our agreement with Hare that important moral issues ought to be approached as objectively as possible with sound reasoning and an ability to weight relevant considerations; nor does it mean that people cannot learn to reason better or that they cannot acquire deeper moral insight or greater sensitivity.

Kohlberg's studies of human moral development support this position. Drawing upon the work of Piaget and using longitudinal, shorter-term and cross-cultural studies, he and his colleagues have established that people progress through a series of hierarchical and invarient stages in their cognitive-moral development, that they markedly differ in the quality and sophistication of their moral reasoning and in the levels of moral orientation they eventually attain. Table 6.1 presents a summary of these moral stages. They should be studied carefully, for several observations need to be made about these stages to establish a basis for understanding the points we wish to raise about this theory and its significance for student accountability.[2]

The two stages falling under the first level of orientation represent what is essentially an egocentric phase in the moral development of people and is usually characteristic of younger children, but these stages also can be represented in the thinking of some adults. The stage 1 person generally defines what is right in terms of the power associated with authority and in terms of the physical consequences attending human actions. The acts which people commit are right or wrong not because others have legitimate rights or interests that ought to be honored, but because of the rewards one receives for approved behavior or the punishment that is likely to attend breaking rules or disobeying authority. At stage 2, self-interest remains paramount but with greater awareness that others have interests to pursue. This stage of orientation would incorporate the element of reciprocity through mutual exchange and agreement. One's self-interest can be promoted by doing something for another person, but if our interpretation is correct, this orientation is more along the lines of "you scratch my back and I will scratch yours" rather than one of altruistic motivation or moral concern for the interests of others.

Level II, conventional morality, represents a significant transition as the individual enters a level of moral reasoning where *shared* feelings,

Table 6.1.
The six stages of moral judgment and development

LEVEL AND STAGE	WHAT IS RIGHT	REASONS FOR DOING RIGHT	SOCIAL PERSPECTIVE OF STAGE
LEVEL I—PRECONVENTIONAL Stage 1—Heteronomous Morality	To avoid breaking rules backed by punishment, obedience for its own sake, and avoiding physical damage to persons and property.	Avoidance of punishment, and the superior power of authorities.	*Egocentric point of view.* Doesn't consider the interests of others or recognize that they differ from the actor's; doesn't relate two points of view. Actions are considered physically rather than in terms of psychological interests of others. Confusion of authority's perspective with one's own.
Stage 2—Individualism, Instrumental Purpose, and Exchange	Following rules only when it is to someone's immediate interest; acting to meet one's own interests and needs and letting others do the same. Right is also what's fair, what's an equal exchange, a deal, an agreement.	To serve one's own needs or interests in a world where you have to recognize that other people have their interests, too.	*Concrete individualistic perspective.* Aware that everybody has his own interest to pursue and these conflict, so that right is relative (in the concrete individualistic sense).
LEVEL II—CONVENTIONAL Stage 3—Mutual Interpersonal Expectations, Relationships, and Interpersonal Conformity	Living up to what is expected by people close to you or what people generally expect of people in your role as son, brother, friend, etc. "Being good" is important and means having good motives, showing concern about others. It also means keeping mutual relationships, such as trust, loyalty, respect and gratitude.	The need to be a good person in your own eyes and those of others. Your caring for others. Belief in the Golden Rule. Desire to maintain rules and authority which support stereotypical behavior.	*Perspective of the individual in relationships with other individuals.* Aware of shared feelings, agreements, and expectations which take primacy over individual interests. Relates points of view through the concrete Golden Rule, putting yourself in the other guy's shoes. Does not yet consider generalized system perspective.
Stage 4—Social System and Conscience	Fulfilling the actual duties to which you have agreed. Laws are to be upheld except in extreme cases where they conflict with other fixed social duties. Right is also contributing to society, the group, or institution.	To keep the institution going as a whole, to avoid the breakdown in the system "if everyone did it," or the imperative of conscience to meet one's defined obligations. (Easily confused with Stage 3 belief in rules and authority; see text.)	*Differentiates societal point of view from interpersonal agreement or motives.* Takes the point of view of the system that defines roles and rules. Considers individual relations in terms of place in the system.

LEVEL AND STAGE	WHAT IS RIGHT	REASONS FOR DOING RIGHT	SOCIAL PERSPECTIVE OF STAGE
LEVEL III—POST-CONVENTIONAL, OR PRINCIPLED Stage 5—Social Contract or Utility and Individual Rights	Being aware that people hold a variety of values and opinions, that most values and rules are relative to your group. These relative rules should usually be upheld, however, in the interest of impartiality and because they are the social contract. Some nonrelative values and rights like *life* and *liberty*, however, must be upheld in any society and regardless of majority opinion.	A sense of obligation to law because of one's social contract to make and abide by laws for the welfare of all and for the protection of all people's rights. A feeling of contractual commitment, freely entered upon, to family, friendship, trust, and work obligations. Concern that laws and duties be based on rational calculation of overall utility, "the greatest good for the greatest number."	*Prior-to-society perspective.* Perspective of a rational individual aware of values and rights prior to social attachments and contracts. Integrates perspectives by formal mechanisms of agreement, contract, objective impartiality, and due process. Considers moral and legal points of view; recognizes that they sometimes conflict and finds it difficult to integrate them.
Stage 6—Universal Ethical Principles	Following self-chosen ethical principles. Particular laws or social agreements are usually valid because they rest on such principles. When laws violate these principles, one acts in accordance with the principle. Principles are universal principles of justice: the equality of human rights and respect for the dignity of human beings as individual persons.	The belief as a rational person in the validity of universal moral principals, and a sense of personal commitment to them.	*Perspective of a moral point of view* from which social arrangements derive. Perspective is that of any rational individual recognizing the nature of morality or the fact that persons are ends in themselves and must be treated as such.

SOURCE: L. Kohlberg, "Moral Stages and Moralization: The Cognitive-Developmental Approach." In *Moral Development and Behavior: Theory, Research, and Social Issues*, pp. 34–35, edited by Thomas Lickona. Copyright © 1976 by Holt, Rinehart and Winston. Reprinted by permission of Holt, Rinehart and Winston.

agreements and expectations take precedence over individual interests. The stage 3 person is psychologically orientated toward the values and expectations of the groups and persons with whom he or she is closely associated. At the same time, the values and expectations which are so much a part of the interpersonal relationships of the stage 3 person remain undifferentiated from the broader social point of view. At stage 4 this orientation is expanded to include fidelity to the rules, laws, values and expectations associated with major institutions and conventional morality. Right actions are those which maintain the system and contribute to society; personal relations are viewed in terms of their place within the system.

Level III involves a range of moral reasoning oriented more toward individual rights and ultimately, at stage 6 around universal ethical principles. The thinking of stage 5 and stage 6 persons evolves from that of earlier stages and therefore incorporates an understanding of those points of view. Whereas the stage 4 person tends to agree with and to be persuaded by majority opinion, the individual at stage 5 believes that values and rights such as those of liberty and life must be upheld regardless of majority opinion. At this stage there is a strong obligation to law which we have stated is true of the stage 4 person but for different reasons. While the stage 4 individual is likely to uphold the law because it is the law and doing so is consonant with conventional morality, the stage 5 person is more likely to reason that laws must be upheld because they are necessary for the welfare of all and for the protection of all people's rights. Interestingly, as this stage summary indicates, the stage 5 person will consider the moral and legal point of view, but understandably has difficulty integrating them when they conflict.

The latter observation offers a point of comparison to distinguish the kind of reasoning which is respectively characteristic of stage 5 and stage 6 persons. Earlier we alluded to the letter which Martin Luther King drafted from jail. The content of this letter is not only instructive, but offers a good example of the differences in reasoning at these stages of moral development.

There is a type of constructive nonviolent tension which is necessary for growth. Just as Socrates felt it was necessary to create a tension in the mind so that individuals could rise from the bondage of half-truths, so must we see the need for nonviolent gadflies to help create the kind of tension in society that will help men rise from the dark depths of prejudice and racism.

One may well ask, "How can you advocate breaking some laws and obeying others?" The answer lies in the fact that there are two types of laws, just and unjust. One has not only a legal but a moral responsibility to obey just laws. One has a moral responsibility to disobey unjust laws. An unjust law is a human law that is not rooted in eternal law and natural law. Any law that uplifts human personality is just, any law that degrades human personality is unjust. An unjust law is a code that a numerical or power majority group compels a minority group to obey but does not make binding on itself. This is difference made legal.

I do not advocate evading or defying the law as would the rabid segregationist. That would lead to anarchy. One who breaks an unjust law must do so openly, lovingly, and with a willingness to accept the penalty. An individual who breaks a law that conscience tells him is unjust, and willingly accepts the penalty of imprisonment in order to arouse the conscience of the community over its injustice, is in reality expressing the highest respect for law.[3]

In defying certain laws, King acted on self-chosen ethical principles he would be willing to universalize; in other words, he would be willing to have others follow similar principles if they were confronted with a similar set of circumstances. Although King was arrested and placed in jail, this was not a common occurance in a life that had been law-abiding. In arguing that just laws ought to be obeyed, King provides evidence of his belief in the institution of law, and he probably would have agreed with the stage 5 person that people normally should work through the system to change undesirable laws. But this was not a typical situation: History had demonstrated that the social practices and laws which King found so oppressive had existed for decades and very likely would continue to exist for a long time. King faced a dilemma in which his personal moral convictions and belief in the law were constantly tested by the reality of the legal and social practices of his time and, as a result, he assigned priority to moral principles over an obedience to laws which he considered demeaning to the human spirit and dignity of his people. King chose a course of action consistent with what he believed to be morally right, but in doing so he did not ask that he be excused from the penalties associated with breaking the law; in this respect he acknowledged the importance and validity of legal institutions while acting according to moral principles which for him overrode laws that were fundamentally unjust from a moral point of view. His reasoning incorporates a strong belief in universal ethical principles characteristic of stage 6 persons; because his actions were based on such principles and were taken at considerable risk to himself in the face of strong opposition, we believe his actions illustrate the meaning of moral autonomy.

The stages depicted by table 6.1 are hierarchical in at least two respects. First, individuals do not arrive at any given stage of moral development without progressing through those which precede it. A given stage necessarily subsumes the reasoning and understanding associated with those which are prior. Second, as individuals progress into higher stages they evidence levels of reasoning which are more sophisticated from the standpoint of individual analysis, and the ability to recognize considerations that are more comprehensive and relevant than are those generally taken into account by persons at earlier stages. This stage hierarchy suggests that a greater degree of intelligence may be necessary for the kind of reasoning that is required at the highest level of moral orientation, i.e., at stage 5 and 6; but while intelligence may be a key factor, it cannot function as an exclusive or a sufficient condition for moral development. In other words, the fact that a person is intelligent offers no guarantee that he or she will acquire a higher degree of moral awareness. In carrying out its mission the Third Reich recruited many people who were intelligent. Albert Speer did not lack intelligence, and in fulfilling the policies of his government he was joined by many people who were engineers, judges, lawyers, medical doctors and craftsmen. Thus, while Kohlberg's studies have established the qualitative patterns of reasoning represented by these stages, his research also indicates that for moral development to occur individual intelligence and reasoning must be focused on moral problems and engaged in the task of trying to resolve normative issues, particularly within a social context that exposes the individual to differing points of view.

The foregoing is evident in the methods Kohlberg employs to determine an individual's level of moral orientation and in the strategies he and his colleagues have utilized to promote moral development and insight. His methods for determining a subject's level of moral orientation often involve situations in which they are asked to respond to a variety of moral dilemmas. These dilemmas are presented through the format of stories in which the central characters must contend with moral problems and resolve them through moral choice and action. After considering the circumstances of a moral dilemma, Kohlberg's subjects are then asked to state what they believe is the right thing to do under the circumstances and why, or to explain why they think a character's actions were right or wrong. In assessing an individual's stage of moral development the fact that a particular moral choice or act is stated to be right or wrong is less important than *why* the subject believes that it is. The moral orientation of people is manifested in the reasons they offer in supporting their position and in the kinds of things they appeal to and consider relevant in justifying their choices.[4]

Other studies by Kohlberg and his followers have shown that progression from any given stage of moral awareness to the next can be facilitated by a carefully planned, structured intervention. Again, this intervention involves posing moral dilemmas, but rather than asking for individual responses within a one-to-one relationship, participants are asked to evaluate moral problems and to state their position and supporting arguments within a context involving group discussion and the moral thinking of other persons. It is important to note that progression from one stage of reasoning to the next cannot be effectively promoted in situations where all of the participants operate at the same stage of moral development. Development occurs when the moral outlooks of the participants differ, and individuals must come to terms with their own beliefs in relation to those held by others. Stage progression is stimulated through the cognitive tension and challenge that differing values and points of view tend to generate, and from an exposure to the thinking associated with higher stages. However, while moral development is not as likely to occur in situations where everyone is at the same stage of reasoning, it also is unlikely to occur where the range of moral orientation is too great. Generally, people at stage 1 cannot assimilate the reasoning or understand the kinds of considerations associated with the thinking of persons at stages 5 and 6; they are more likely to be receptive to the position of persons operating at stage 2, stage 2 persons to that of persons at stage 3, and so forth. Consequently, to be effective in promoting moral development, Kohlberg's group discussions require a structured membership and must follow procedures based on principles that have evolved from his studies; moreover, they must be guided by persons who are knowledgeable about such principles and well trained in cognitive-moral development theory.[5]

We stated that many studies have established the qualitative differences in moral reasoning represented by these stages and that other studies involving an application of Kohlberg's findings have shown that moral development can be promoted by using strategies which expose an individual at any given level of moral orientation to the reasoning characteristic of the next hierarchical stage. A great deal has been written about Kohlberg's research, and understandably this theory has its critics. For example, one very important issue is the degree of correlation between the actual behavior of people and the level of moral development they evidence by their verbal responses to situational moral dilemmas. In facing difficult moral situations, do stage 6 persons usually behave in ways that are just and fair, that is, in a manner consistent with universal ethical principles, and do they demonstrate the degree of personal autonomy one would expect from persons whose stated position is to follow principles that are self-chosen, even if it means going against majority or conventional opinion? The same can be said of the other stages as well. Do stage 1 and stage 2 persons usually behave in ways that are consistent with what they contend makes any given set of actions right or wrong?

From a methodological standpoint, the task of researching and establishing valid correlations between moral behavior and moral reasoning is extremely difficult. One simply cannot follow subjects every moment and always be present to study the responses they make to real-life moral problems, particularly when such problems arise spontaneously in the course of their lives. Even if this were possible, there would be the additional problem of trying to determine which are the most significant among numerous factors that could be influencing a person's behavior on any particular occasion. However, the improved rates of recidivism found among prison inmates participating in Kohlberg's moral development programs is encouraging, and we believe it provides evidence that people do behave in ways consistent with their moral orientation.[6] Critics have questioned whether this improvement should be attributed to a higher level of moral orientation on the part of Kohlberg's subjects or simply to the additional attention they received as a result of participating in his programs. Increased personal attention can elicit cooperation and interest, but personal attention alone cannot provide the additional cognitive insight or a more advanced understanding of moral questions that inmate participants evidenced during their involvement in these programs and prior to their release from prison. In other words, changes in their moral outlook resulted at least as much from the nature and content of the attention they received as from the mere fact of its occurrence.

Undoubtedly, the degree to which moral behavior correlates with moral reasoning is a function of many social and personal factors, but despite the problems attending this type of research, there is sufficient evidence to indicate that the values, beliefs and moral orientation of the individual are significant among such factors. We may not have the assurance that stage 6 persons will always act in a manner that is autonomous and consistent with universal ethical principles, but we believe they are more likely to evidence such behavior than persons who lack a basic understanding of these principles and as a consequence fail to grasp what the latter really require of a person. In this respect we believe there is a connection between behavior and what people rationally comprehend; that persons who acquire a sense of fairness, who come to understand the principles of freedom and justice are more likely to have a commitment to such principles and to behave accordingly. Similarly, we assume that persons who are morally oriented to the thinking characteristic of stages 1 and 2 will be more likely to behave in ways that evidence a deference to the power associated with authority, to act primarily out of regard for the rewards and punishments which attend their behavior and the promotion of their own interests, and that they will do so whether such behavior compromises the legitimate interests of others or happens to be morally right or wrong for other reasons.

The assumptions and strategies of Kohlberg's theory differ markedly from those associated with operant conditioning. Earlier we outlined several criticisms in relation to Skinner's theory of human behavior, at the same time acknowledging that operant conditioning is a factor in behavior at all ages. Skinner's recommendations for modifying behavior are appropriate and very effective in certain situations, particularly in changing the behavior of persons operating at lower stages of moral awareness where Kohlberg has found that decisions about what is right or wrong are based almost exclusively on a consideration of the rewards and punishments attending behavior. In addition, we recognize that practically everyone responds to positive reinforcement and that praise and various forms of reward represent an important consideration in our lives. The fact that reinforcement can be effective in motivating people and in modifying their behavior is by no means incompatible with Kohlberg's findings. But the preceding can be acknowledged without accepting Skinner's assumption that reinforcement and conditioning are the only factors that play a role in shaping behavior or are the only factors which influence a person's behavior on any given occasion, particularly the behavior of people who are consistent in demonstrating a greater degree of moral insight in their reasoning.

Our disagreement with Skinner to this point has centered on a rejection of this assumption, but it really involves two additional concerns. First, from a practical standpoint what does operant conditioning really have to offer to anyone who possesses a reasonable degree of intelligence? It is a simple fact that when used in isolation reinforcement only tells a person that certain forms of behavior are approved or not approved *by others;* it does not provide any insight as to *why* they should be approved or disapproved, why certain actions for forms of behavior are desirable or undesirable or why they may be right or wrong. Even persons entering a program of behavior modification to break an addictive habit, such as smoking, at least know *why* they are entering it. True, they may feel a sense of failure in not having sufficient will power to stop, but they have reasons for wanting to end their addiction that go beyond reinforcement. People who have struggled with problems similar to this know that more is involved in the cause than simple conditioning, although certain behavioral factors and attendant changes in habit and the contexts of their environment may be key elements that must be understood if they are to overcome their dependence and effect a lasting change.

Our second concern is closely related and, for purposes of this study, equally significant. It has to do with the role operant conditioning would assign to students as they try to cope with the personal and social problems that occur throughout their lives. In postulating that behavior can be modified only by manipulating the environment, and in denying the element of personal choice, this theory absolves the individual of any responsibility and sets the stage for several related assumptions that carry serious implications for the way in which we approach the learning of youth and their accountability. Skinner assumes that the responsibility for deciding what society should be like, what should be valued and which kinds of behavior will be acceptable or unacceptable, must necessarily reside in the domain of behavioral psychologists because of their presumed expertise. Consistent with this assumption, Skinner prescribes behaviors which he believes are desirable for building a better world, and he would implement conditioning strategies to bring about the behavioral changes he values, but must an individual be knowledgeable about operant conditioning theory to deal with these issues? The focus of this theory is not on the individual and what he or she might offer or become in the process of attempting to understand and deal with such questions; on the contrary, since personal choice is only an illusion, the thinking, judgment and beliefs of the individual are irrelevant and therefore have no role where personal behavior and normative issues are concerned.

Given these assumptions, if the behavior of our youth is to be modified exclusively through the mechanism of a contrived environment where influences of change are external to themselves and beyond their involvement, would it not follow that throughout their lives there would always have to be someone other than they to decide what is right or preferable, to direct their lives and condition what they are to be? And if this is to be the case, how will they acquire the adaptability, the reasoning and problem-solving skills necessary to cope with external processes of change which appear to be accelerating and so endemic to modern life? The behaviorist may argue that personal abilities similar to the above are unnecessary in the scientific world of operant conditioning and within communities and a general society patterned after Walden; perhaps, but we doubt that in the future there will be enough behavioral psychologists with sufficient knowledge to address the economic, social and political problems of this world on all fronts.

Because we reject the belief that environmental response is the only factor that determines behavior and with it the related notions that people never have a choice in or any responsibility for what they do, we assume that students have a responsibility where their learning and behavior are concerned. Obviously, our position on this question involves a different set of assumptions about how to modify the attitudes and behavior of students and how one should approach their learning and accountability. In attempting the former, we too must have beliefs about appropriate and inappropriate behavior and ideals about a better world, but the difference between our position and that of the behaviorist centers on our belief in what individuals can learn and offer in the process of trying to resolve such questions and in what the individual can do in translating a deeper insight and decisions into action. Students have a stake in the problems and activities of this society, and because their thinking and feelings influence their choices and affect the quality of life for others around them, we assume that students must be involved in trying to understand their behavior as well as the same problems and issues that concern Skinner and other adults. Operant conditioning strategies are admittedly effective in dealing with particular kinds of behavior, but as a theory it fails to acknowledge the role that individuals must play if our present and future problems are to be resolved or at least managed more effectively. Our youth should be encouraged to examine what others believe and value in relation to their own values and beliefs. They need frank discussions about issues that are of concern to their generation as well as to this nation, for these issues and the challenges they present are a part of reality and having an understanding of reality is important to the development of a person and in some respects can be crucial to his survival.

Accountability for behavior

In contrast to Skinner, who essentially views behavior as a series of predetermined reactions to environmental response, Kohlberg's research identifies other behavioral elements. These include the ways in which people interpret and reason about the content of experience and the manner in which this interaction is manifested in their moral orientation and outlook. For Skinner, the student would appear to be an entity devoid of any feelings that have behavioral significance, powerless in the face of what the environment determines him or her to be; an entity to be acted upon by others and, however reflective, insignificant both cognitively and as a participant in matters which involve personal direction and the world in which it must occur. On the other hand, Kohlberg's strategies involve engaging a person's mind and reasoning in the task of trying to resolve moral issues that are a part of everyday life. In this respect Kohlberg provides an approach to youth that recognizes the reality of their world and the significance of their intelligence and responsibility within it.

Kohlberg's research is important because it identifies elements that influence our moral outlook and provides strategies that can be effective in promoting moral development. But for purposes of this study, the additional value of his research resides in the direction it can point us in developing approaches to student accountability and in providing a structure for accountability relationships in general. Several features of accountability identified in this study closely parallel the central elements of Kohlberg's theory. For moral growth and development to occur, Kohlberg postulates the necessity for social interaction where the values and moral beliefs of the individual are measured in relation to those held by others. Putting aside those occasions in which we may feel a certain accountability to our personal conscience, the concept of accountability by its nature implies a relationship of two or more parties where accounting for responsibilities is the issue and various requirements, expectations and individual points of view play a role.

The social interaction and personal involvement associated with Kohlberg's approach are very much a part of accountability relationships, as are the rational and cognitive elements that are a primary focus of his theory. In our initial chapters several distinctions were drawn in relation to the forms of accounting that people are expected to provide. Several of these forms of accounting were stated to be a central feature of communication, and their parallels with rational procedure and the aims of education were noted. In saying that schools should cultivate the ability of students to adequately account for themselves, more is implied than simply answering to others about the things for which one is responsible. When an individual is called upon to provide an explanation of complex matters or to offer a justification for actions that he or she may have taken in their regard, meaningful communication will often require personal introspection, an analysis of problems, facts and events, the abilities to perceive relationships, to think clearly and logically about what is given and expected—abilities and dispositions that are a function of human cognition and reasoning. Kohlberg's methods require that people explain and justify the moral positions they adopt, and in many cases so do the requirements imposed within accountability relationships.

Because of these common elements we wish to advance a position that admittedly may be new and, from the standpoint of research and practice, clearly warrants more attention. We believe that a mutuality and synergetic relationship exist between the moral development of youth and the experiences associated with their accountability. Our argument may repeat previously stated themes, but it will clarify the interaction that we see between the moral orientation of people and the ways in which we hold them accountable. On the one hand, we noted that in moral situations the reasoning and moral orientation of the individuals involved will very much determine how they view and ultimately address their responsibilities and obligations, and that the actions they take or fail to take in regard to the latter generally establish the nature and occasions of their accountability. People who are morally insensitive to the rights of others and who frequently disregard them for personal interests may find themselves being held accountable before the law and other authorities for actions which are seldom committed by persons who have acquired this moral sensitivity and who generally behave in ways that reflect a basic respect for the rights of others. Furthermore, our analysis indicates that when accountability relationships are established, the probability of compliance with whatever they require is a function of the individual's moral outlook and how the individual or group interprets the obligation. For these reasons, the moral orientation of the individual remains a primary factor in the concept of accountability.

On the other hand, in saying that the moral orientation and accountability of youth involve a synergetic relationship, we mean that the ways in which adults handle situations of student accountability represent a factor that either will contribute to their moral insight and development or will be ineffective or even detrimental where they are concerned. Whether the issue is the responsibilities they are expected to fulfill or personal acts they may have committed, the manner in which we hold students accountable and the requirements we impose will influence their values and moral outlook. If we are correct in taking this position and Kohlberg's research has the degree of validity we assume, then different approaches to student accountability may be necessary and the concept itself may have to be viewed in a different light.

Kohlberg provides tools that can be utilized to facilitate moral development. His methods involve group settings and procedures which are fairly structured, and his research demonstrates their effectiveness. But for most persons, the influences which contribute to the arrest or promotion of their moral development are a function of experiences that are extremely varied in origin. These influences are to be found within adult and peer relationships, the environment of the home, neighborhood, school and work, and in the many contexts of informal social activities. They often occur within a stream of experience that is fairly unstructured, and many of these influences are seemingly incidental in nature, but they also occur in situations where experiences are more contrived, as would be the case when a person participates in church discussion groups or the group processes associated with Kohlberg's theory.

In the final analysis, within this total realm of personal experience the important factor is the quality of such influences and whether a sufficient number involve elements Kohlberg has identified. Children are not born with prejudice and a hatred of minorities, persons who are gay or who are in some identifiable respect different from what they believe themselves to be; their prejudice is an acquired outlook. Its seeds can be sown within the context of the home and the environment of a neighborhood and culture, but whether or not it will remain throughout their lives depends to a large extent on whether or not they are exposed to points of view, values, and modes of thought that are different. For these reasons, we believe that certain elements and strategies associated with Kohlberg's theory are relevant even within situations and relationships that are less structured, and that this is equally true in many contexts where students are expected to be accountable for their behavior.

An example involving a problem of student discipline will illustrate the point we are making. Take the fairly straightforward case of a student who is habitually late at a school that expects its students to arrive in the morning on time for the beginning of classes. Many schools hold students accountable for such behavior by issuing detention slips and requiring them to stay after school for a certain period of time. The time that must be given by the student represents a forfeiture of personal freedom to do other things. The detention requirement and the attendant loss of freedom it imposes are a form of punishment for violations of the school policy. It seems obvious that throughout their lives students will be expected to show up for work on time and to keep apppointments, whether they involve going to the dentist or keeping a promise to meet a friend at a particular time and place. Our relationships with others involve these obligations, and our attitudes about them are formed during our youth. In the present case we shall not debate the issue of whether or not students should be expected to arrive on time, for we take this as a given. But there are several things that need to be said about the accountability of the student in this example.

First, it is a relationship of accountability. We noted that people can be held accountable and answerable for their behavior through forms of accounting that are more stringent and essentially punitive in nature. Skinner would contend that this approach involves an aversive form of conditioning. In other words, the school responds to undesirable behavior by punishing the student. He would prefer to have the student's behavior modified through means involving positive reinforcement, and would contend that in the long run the latter will prove to be more effective. In some respects we agree and disagree with this position.

Although aversive, we do not find humane and reasonable forms of punishment to be categorically undesirable or believe that they are ineffective in changing the behavior of people. The constraint on freedom under this attendance policy does represent a form of punishment, but its imposition at least has the value of giving a clear indivation of what is and is not approved in regard to student behavior. Within a school population there are students who generally do not "get into trouble." For the most part they present few if any behavior problems, but like other students their age, they may occasionally try to test the system or the expectations of their parents or the school. When this occurs in the home, if they are fortunate to have family relationships which involve security and mutual respect, where there is a sharing of values and points of view, a brief discussion, a disapproving glance or even the temporary denial of a privilege may be all that is necessary to have them come to terms with what is and is not acceptable in relation to what they have done or may propose to do. More than one parent has ordered the return of keys to the family car and done so with positive results, although it is a form of punishment. In the school, one afternoon's detention may be all that is required to alter the behavior of such a student. Its effectiveness may be due to the embarrassment a generally conscientious student may feel, to the loss of freedom or to the boredom experienced in the detention room, or to the student's eventual realization, preferably after a brief discussion, that the policy is necessary because classes would be constantly interrupted if people were permitted to wander in at will. Our point is simply this: Even "good" students occasionally try to see what they "can get by with," may come late or skip school to be with a friend on a joint adventure, or may simply test the system to see if anyone cares. The strategies of a disapproving glance, the denial of certain privileges or issuing a detention slip may be forms of punishment, but they can be effective and are better than doing nothing, for they at least provide some direction and structure at a time in life when such guidelines are often needed.

In contrast, some youth are out at all hours engaging in activities that are detrimental to themselves and to others. Far too many get the message that no one really cares because they experience little reaction from parents and other adults and, as a consequence, they often turn inward or to peers and others who are involved in the same activities. There are parents and educators who will be angered by this observation, and with some justification. They will remember occasions when they made a great deal of effort, invested considerable caring and trust in trying to redirect a young person bent on destruction, only to have that person fulfill his or her mission. These experiences involve strong feelings, disappointment and sometimes considerable pain, and many of us have had them. Some students simply will not make it despite the efforts of conscientious adults, but it does not follow that because this is true for some, it is uniformly true for all. Many students do respond in positive ways to adult interest and guidance. The real question before us in this chapter is whether there are approaches to student accountability and behavior that are more effective in providing the guidance that is needed and in promoting moral growth and the deeper understanding it requires.

But Skinner is correct in other respects. There is a difference between the occasional use of punishment and situations where punishment is the only approach used by parents, the school or other adults who happen to be part of a young persons's life. When used in isolation and as the *only* approach to student problems, punishment is undesirable. Take the present case. The student in question is being held accountable for his behavior through the same form of accountability that we stated might be very effective with another student who has a different orientation, that is, through a form of punishment that involves being kept after school. But he is habitually late. This student has been issued a constant series of detention slips, and no doubt some have been given because he has even skipped detention. His indebtedness at this point is staggering— after compounding he owes 110 detentions, and with only 50 days remaining in the school year, it is possible that he will have to come during the summer. If the purpose of this accountability relationship is to do more than indicate what the school approves and disapproves, if it is to have as a part of its purpose promoting a change in behavior that is based on the thinking, outlook and attitudes of the student as we believe it should, then it is obviously failing its purpose.

The student in this example is based on a real-life counterpart. He and his school shall remain anonymous, but what happened to him will be helpful in illustrating a principle that ought to govern any accountability relationship: namely, that the ways in which we expect people to be accountable ought to serve the basic purposes of the accountability relationships in which they are involved. In the case in question, school officials began an intensive review of the student's history and invested some time in talking with him. This student had committed numerous offenses, some rather serious, and after two suspensions from school he was on the brink of permanent expulsion. In other words, tardiness was only one of several problems; this was a tough case and a tough student. The conversations that ensued explored his behavior and its harm to himself as well as to the rights and interests of others. They revealed personal feelings about himself and his relationships within his family and with his peers. His school record was one of repeated failure, and subsequent evaluations indicated extreme difficulty in reading. The repeated failures made sense. He lacked the skills that success in traditional academic classes required. But the failures left their mark, and so did the problems at home. The picture was not pleasant. The school had encountered and come to know a student who essentially did not respect rules and authority or the rights of others because he did not respect himself. What should be done with him?It was obvious that he would never attend college, and expulsion was certainly a tempting way out. To some, the solution in this case seemed simple: He was one student among many, and because they had been aggravated by his constant irritations—and they were constant—he was expendable. But putting aside its moral implications, this was a shallow solution. The detention hall was populated with a significant number of students who were very similar to our friend; many had experienced frequent failure in school and to a large extent in their general life; and some were responding with behavior that was equally disrupting and obnoxious.

The particular school in this case was fairly innovative, a fact that was evident in the variety and comprehensiveness of its programs. Fortunately, the school principal, many of its teachers, the superintendent of the school system and the members of the school board to whom he reported were people who cared about students and were receptive to programs designed to serve their needs. Even more fortunate, the citizens and taxpayers of the community usually supported their efforts. The school began a program of work-study for this group of students and others who were not as troubled but who also were unlikely to attend college. Their academic program involved emphasis on improving basic skills, making reports and presentations before groups, filling out applications, participating in personal interviews, and writing letters and vitae. Counselors were hired to supervise the performance of these students in relation to their places of employment. In this program students acquired a new set of responsibilities, and they were certainly held accountable for them. At one level, their accountability involved a weekly check-off and written evaluations of their work performance. These included whether or not they showed up on time, performed assigned tasks, took initiative on the job; how they related to other employees, work supervisors and so forth. At another level, their accountability included a requirement that they participate in regular discussions which focused on problems that individual students were having at work, their points of view about such things as interpersonal relationships, how they felt about themselves, their program and the school, their values, and various social and moral issues.

With the support of the school and their employers, the students in this program formed an organization. We shall not dwell on its purpose and activities except to say that by the conclusion of the first year our troublesome detention student had been elected its president. When the group sponsored a spring dinner to thank their employers, he stood before his fellow students and his teachers in coat and tie, and with a self-confidence and poise that were surprising to many who "remembered him when," he opened the ceremonies by introducing the most prominent people in town.

This story has a successful ending. It may not be typical, but it is nevertheless true. The lesson we can learn is that in holding students accountable for their behavior, not all forms of accounting will be effective or suitable for serving the basic purposes we hope to achieve. In this situation the accountability of these students had evolved from detention slips and often contentious and superficial encounters with school officials, to accountability relationships which centered on a different set of responsibilities and which involved different expectations about the ways in which they should be accountable for them. Students, like most of us, seldom change overnight, and several students in this program were held accountable through means of punishment. After repeated warnings and discussions, a few were dropped from the program, and some among them dropped out of school. In the earlier stages, a few had to be warned or placed on probation with the threat of similar action. But this was not true for the vast majority with whom they later progressed.

Positive reinforcements were a significant factor. Students were paid for working. Other reinforcements came in the form of praise, good evaluations, better relationships with adults and, for most students, a sense of success. The quality and nature of the relationships between these students and the adults to whom they were accountable were an equally important factor. For the most part, their relationships came to involve greater respect for the value of discussion, for sharing ideas and having the opportunity to express and challenge opinions. Interviews with supervisors and students alike indicated that a majority felt positive about their experience and had been significantly affected by what it involved. In other words, these students still had to deal with adult expectations, but they often did so in forums of mutual interest and discussion, where the opportunity to express how one thought about things was accepted and everyone, including their supervisors, had to come to terms with the thinking of others. Undoubtedly, some of these occasions were discomforting, but they resulted in a measure of growth and maturing that were quite evident in the rate of graduation among a group of students who had been destined to drop out of school. Interestingly, the change in outlook of these students was evident in their job performance to an extent that more than 90 percent were employed after graduation by the same companies that had closely observed them over a period of many months.

The manner in which these students were expected to be accountable involved forms of accounting that varied from situations in which they related and reported their activities to contexts in which a few experienced negative response and punishment. But despite the range of accountability expected in these relationships, for all of the students in this program there were many occasions in which emphasis was placed on requiring them to explain and to justify actions they had taken in regard to other people as well as their personal responsibilities. However incidental or contrived these occasions may have been, and however inadequate their opinions and beliefs may have seemed at the time, opportunities were provided for other people to listen to these students, to scrutinize and respond to their ideas and feelings about things that mattered most to them at that particular time in their lives. These relationships involved a concern for trying to understand, asking "why," and, when reasons, excuses and opinions were given, appraising their adequacy. In essence, whether their accountability occurred in one-to-one relationships or in the social context of group discussions, it embodied a number of elements central to the position of Kohlberg as well as of Skinner, and there were elements that were quite consistent with other theories of human behavior: for example, the degree to which such things as self-actualization, experiencing achievement and success and seeing value in what we do influence self-respect, whether or not we basically like ourselves, and ultimately how the latter can affect the ways in which we view and treat other people.

It is important to distinguish particular accountability transactions—that is, the exchange and expectations associated with any given occasion—from the longer-term accountability relationships of which they are a part. Our accountability to the IRS involves a relationship extending over many years, and it is one that requires numerous accountability transactions. Accountability to our family or to an employer can involve relationships of some duration and be comprised of many occasions where we are expected to be accountable for a variety of matters. Consequently, it is our position that the forms of accounting people are expected to provide ought not only to be suitable for what seems to be required or necessary on any particular occasion, but that their collective or aggregate effect should also serve the ultimate goals of the relationship itself. We stated that the foregoing principle ought to govern any accountability relationship, but where students are concerned it is especially important, whether we happen to be dealing with the behavior of a typically "good" student, the behavior of our detention student or that of the chronic delinquent. Childhood and adolescence represent a formative period during which youth occupy a position of considerable dependence. The accountability procedures adopted in their regard must be selected to deal with particular situations, but in the long run they must involve a body of strategies that have the effect of promoting moral development and providing for students a better understanding of how their actions, moral outlook and values not only affect others around them but in large measure define who they are as people and determine the meaning that will be associated with their lives.

The forms of accounting discussed in this study as well as others may be required in their endeavor to achieve such ends. It is in this sense that we believe an effective concept of accountability for youth presupposes not only an application of Kohlberg's strategies but also at times those of Skinner and others, strategies that are appropriate for the occasion and for the particular level of development at which the individual is functioning. Chronic delinquents offer a case in point. A delinquent who is responsible for repeated acts of vandalism reflects values and a moral outlook devoid of sensitivity to the property rights of other persons and to the cost, inconvenience and hardship that his actions impose. His accountability before authorities no doubt will involve restrictions on freedom or the denial of privileges, but if our objective in treating him is to provide more than custodial care and to promote the personal understanding and development we have been discussing, other approaches will be required, especially if he is to acquire an appreciation for the rights of other persons. One approach could involve placing him in a program of work-study and to require that a portion of his earnings be paid as restitution to his victim or in some manner contributed to other victims of vandalism. Having to put in x amount of work and hours to earn x amount of dollars and then having to forfeit a portion of his earnings for this purpose may bring him closer to understanding the value of things, what they cost in terms of personal effort and why people are inconvenienced, angered, and feel a sense of personal violation when acts of vandalism occur.

Although we believe a program of this sort would have value and be a step in the right direction, opportunities also must be provided for discussion and the kinds of examination of ideas and beliefs that have proven to be effective in Kohlberg's research and in the school we described. Furthermore, our delinquent might acquire a greater measure of self-respect and a deeper appreciation for the value of other people in his life if his working and making restitution were augmented by the requirement that he participate in a program similar to Outward Bound, where individual skills and abilities are tested in specific and challenging situations, and where one must learn to work with others if common goals are to be achieved. Some may argue that these approaches do not represent forms of accounting and holding youth accountable. We disagree. The basic problem should not be obscured: We are talking about a chronic delinquent. His participation in such programs can be required as a part of his accountability and treatment, and we believe that in the long run to make such a requirement would prove more effective than simply providing him with food and a place to sleep. Requiring his involvement in programs of this nature does represent an infringement of freedom, but infringement of freedom is not uncommon in a society that sees value in promoting important causes.

People inducted into the armed services encounter and must deal with a range of experiences defined by their drill instructor and other military personnel, and precious few have any sense of personal freedom or discretion in the matter. The methods used in basic training are designed to bring recruits to an acceptable level of physical fitness, to ensure that they will be ready for combat and have the skills necessary to fulfill certain responsibilities. Some of the strategies used in their training may be irritating or seem senseless, but what matters is whether on balance the full complement of strategies used in their training provides experiences that promote the attainment of ends which are justified and considered desirable. Accountability relationships are similar in having basic purposes to be served, and where these purposes are justified, methods or forms of accounting ought to be selected that have the effects of promoting their fulfillment.

Accountability for learning

Our discussion has focused on the issue of student accountability in relation to behavior, but the foregoing principle is relevant in situations where they are expected to be accountable for what they learn. Furthermore, it is highly relevant to the accountability of their teachers. The performance-contracting arrangements proposed for education actually require two levels of accountability. The more obvious is that of the teacher or contractor who is either rewarded or not rewarded as a function of student performance. At the same time, by establishing performance objectives and testing students for achievement, we really expect students to provide an accounting of their competence in relation to such objectives. Even in the absence of performance-contracting arrangements, evaluating and assessing student achievement have been regarded as necessary instructional tools for years, and in this respect so has student accountability for learning. Consistency with the foregoing principle would require that the various forms of accounting expected from students serve the objectives and purposes which underlie an evaluation of their learning. For example, if all that is desired in expecting a student to give an account of the Civil War is that she be able to relate correct dates, names and places, then testing her for such knowledge could probably be accomplished through the use of multiple-choice tests.

Without question, knowledge of such facts is relevant to saying that a person knows something about the Civil War. But if the student is expected to offer an explanation of the primary factors and conditions that contributed to the Civil War, and to justify her position, then something different is expected in relation to her learning. The latter expectation clearly requires that a student go beyond a relation of historical facts and try to analyze, understand and present a position as to why they occurred; consequently, other forms of accounting may be more suitable.

Our second point is that students have a primary responsibility in relation to their learning. The content and processes of thought, as well as knowledge and understanding, reside in the mind, and ultimately whatever changes we seek to influence in the way a person thinks or reasons, and in what he or she may understand, must occur within the individual. To pretend that parents and teachers are solely responsible for learning ignores this consideration and is undesirable from the standpoint of the student and the society of which he is a part. In absolving students of personal responsibility for either their learning or behavior, we dimnish their dignity and set a convenient stage for innumerable excuses. If they are encouraged to believe that their lives are entirely contingent upon others, then when the inevitable disappointments and failures occur that are a part of life, there will always be someone or something else to blame. In stressing this point, by no means do we wish to deny the responsibilities that adults have in regard to youth. By virtue of their authority and the positions they hold in relation to children and through their decisions, choices and actions, adults largely determine the opportunities and enrichment that children will or will not have in their experience.

But the position that students have a responsibility for learning is seldom discussed or recognized in many proposals for educational accountability. In the next chapter we shall examine the basic assumption that teachers are responsible for learning and therefore should be held more accountable for student performance. Teachers do have important responsibilities in relation to their profession and the learning of students, but the nature of their responsibility must be clarified where their accountability is concerned and recognition given to the fact that others share in this responsibility.

CHAPTER 7

Teacher accountability:
three basic issues

This study has examined the primary elements of accountability and identified several conditions that must be recognized if practical applications of this concept are to involve meaningful and effective relationships. The reader has been asked to consider the nature of various forms of accounting and their relationship to educational objectives, to explore the moral and legal basis for obligations, and to examine the roles of responsibility and entitlement in establishing such relationships. The subjects of moral development and orientation were introduced in conjunction with other factors because of their respective influence on the ways in which people view their obligations and because of their bearing on the subject of agent compliance. We have adopted the general principle that selected forms of accounting and the manner in which people are expected to be accountable ought to be fair and consistent with the basic purposes of the accountability relationships in which they are involved. Moreover, it is our contention that the elements and principles outlined in this study are relevant to any accountability relationship, including those which involve students and teachers in the field of education. It is for these reasons and in light of our discussion that we now turn to the subject of teacher accountability.

Demands for greater accountability in education and the proposals that accompany them are often directed at teachers. Our initial response to this position focused on performance contracting and questioned its suitability for many aims in education that are fairly indeterminate yet worthwhile to pursue. Despite our concern with this issue, we noted that the functions of evaluating and reporting student progress are necessary in teaching and essential to the processes which promote student learning. There are four elements in the performance-contracting approach to accountability: (1) establishing a fairly definitive set of performance or learning objectives; (2) evaluating or measuring student progress toward such objectives over a period of time; (3) reporting student progress as measured; and (4) either assigning or withholding rewards on the basis of such performance.

Teachers should and in reality must formulate learning and performance objectives for their students: but before teachers can develop appropriate objectives and establish a sensible plan for teaching, they must be knowledgeable about skill development and the skill levels at which their students are functioning. This is especially true during the early and middle years of schooling, when basic skills must be acquired in reading, writing and computation, and when an understanding of fundamental concepts must be established in relation to the various physical and social sciences.

Measurement and evaluation provide the primary means by which we determine student competence in these areas. When educators fail to apply evaluation techniques or ignore their results, serious consequences can occur, leading to frustration, failure or even boredom on the part of the students. The child who functions at a second-grade level in skill development is bound to fail or to be extremely frustrated if given a steady diet of learning material two grade levels beyond his or her present level of functioning; and at the other extreme there is justification of indifference to classroom learning when bright students must contend with subject matter and materials that are unchallenging and well below their level of ability. The concept of individualized instruction embodies the fundamental precepts that teaching objectives should fit the child and that the methods used for their attainment should be designed either to strengthen a given level of performance or to move a child to the next stage of development. Without question, testing and other forms of student evaluation are crucial to this effort.

In the process of reporting or offering an explanation about student performance to students, their parents or to the school administration, teachers are involved with forms of accounting, and when the obligation to provide such an accounting can be established on professional grounds, we contend that teachers are being accountable in relation to such matters. As stated before, those who argue for teacher accountability often neglect the fact that evaluating and reporting student progress have been key functions in education for many years, and to the extent that they have been carried out, students and their teachers have been accountable.

Despite the foregoing, advocates of performance contracting and other accountability proposals could offer a counterargument to our position structured along the following lines:

1. The author appears to agree that the first three elements in performance contracting are necessary in education, and in advocating performance contracting we can see that reporting student progress is a form of accountability. Nevertheless, the incidence of student failure and poor performance on achievement tests clearly demonstrates that merely reporting student progress is insufficient to assure the same degree of success and achievement in education that have been characteristic of business; hence, a more effective form of accountability is required.
2. In the first chapter of this study, the author's own analysis indicates that various forms of accounting exist and that it is possible to hold persons answerable in a manner which extends beyond merely reporting events to include punitive measures and other forms of accountability involving some manner of loss to the accountant.

3. Rather than adopting punitive measures, performance contracting simply incorporates the additional element of an incentive in the form of rewards for results achieved. By an offering these rewards to students and teachers, we encourage and reinforce more effective efforts in achieving results. True, when rewards are withheld, this does represent a loss to the student, teacher or contractor, but it is consistent with the earlier analysis, and in making teachers or contractors more answerable in this manner , performance contracting involves a higher degree of accountability, one designed to produce better results.

The additional element of offering or withholding rewards contingent upon results does represent a different and perhaps even stronger form of accountability than simply reporting student progress. The real issue is not performance contracting per se, but whether or not any given proposal for accountability would be desirable as an educational practice. In our view the suitability of any accountability arrangement would involve three considerations. They are summarized below as basic criteria that we believe should be recognized in any accountability relationship. In essence, the purposes, arrangements and expected forms of accounting associated with such relationships should be:

1. ethically justifiable;
2. based on causal responsibility for the acts, events or occurrences at issue and/or on expectational responsibilities that are reasonable to expect and consistent with the role or performances with which they are associated;
3. suitable for the basic purposes for which the accountability relationship exists and practical in the sense that they can be applied and will yield what they are expected to provide.

The requirement that accountability relationships ought to be ethically justifiable is certainly relevant to the methods we employ in the process of motivating teachers and students, particularly when these methods are incorporated within the accountability process itself. We acknowledged the fact that positive reinforcement in the form of praise, rewards and other incentives is an important consideration in human relationships and can be effective in promoting greater effort and achievement. But these incentives must be used sensibly; when they become the exclusive reason for learning or trying to be an effective teacher, very real issues surface concerning the values we impart to students and what such strategies really say about the motivation of students and their teachers.

Responsibility for learning: the problem of undetermined influences

However, the problems associated with many proposals for teacher accountability go much deeper and involve other criteria and principles we have suggested. The first and second issues we shall discuss relate directly to the problem of establishing causal responsibility for learning and raise questions concerning the expectational responsibilities associated with the role of teaching. The third issue has to do more with the manner in which we hold teachers accountable and whether or not there are forms of accounting that may be more productive throughout all levels of education in dealing with the problems of student performance. Achieving better results in education is certainly desirable. In their role as students and eventually as adults, youth must contend with a complex society, the welfare of which will very much depend on their competency, their values and the kinds of people they become as adults. Their education and the adult roles they must assume in maintaining this culture involve a cross-generational responsibility. Whether or not they will acquire the competencies and values necessary to fulfill these various roles will depend, as it always has, on the opportunities and experiences the present adult generation is willing to provide. But we question whether American business should be embraced as a model for achieving whatever it is we believe students should become or be able to do as adults. As noted before, in a number of respects American business has not been successful, but it is inappropriate as a comparative model for other reasons.

Most of the results that concern business are determinate by nature and therefore particularly suited for measurement, control, standardization and high predictability. Much the same can be said of the means to their existence. The materials processed to bring any product to an intended state are relatively fixed, since their special properties and arrangement are necessary for that state to exist and, once known, can repeatedly be selected to ensure that it will occur time and time again. To recognize this in no way ignores the fact that where a new product is involved, a great deal of trial and error may be necessary in its development; but rather, it suggests that the product's eventual existence will attest to an understanding of basic principles and causal relationships that govern the proper combination of its constituent elements. The "zero-defect" standard to which these proposals refer is possible because materials and physical processes behave according to rules and principles which are themselves essentially determinate and stable—considerations enabling the technician to have control over most if not all variables essential to producing a given result, and which particularly favor an understanding of the causes underlying any failure of its occurrence.

But the characteristics which allow precision and the assurance of results in manufacturing are present to a very limited degree in education. On the one hand, it is possible to apply more than one strategy in reaching a desired outcome. Children have learned to read and write under the more traditional techniques of drill and rote memorization, through what amounts to a fairly passive, teacher-centered learning relationship. But they also have acquired these shills through progressive methods involving student participation and independent as well as group inquiry. Admittedly, some teaching methods may prove more effective than others in achieving a particular set of outcomes, but for the present we cannot say that process A or A alone *will always* lead to a given result, as is frequently the case in industrial production.

Research into educational opportunity indicates that this is true because the variables assisting or impeding educational strategies are numerous, varied, only partially contrived and not as easily understood or controlled. Whatever the mode of teaching selected, the alterations to be made are not in some tangible material, but in the attitudes, beliefs, perceptions and judgments of the learner—behavioral factors far more remote and complex from the standpoint of causality than the factors involved in an industrial process.

As it turns out, the foregoing really offers a point of agreement. Many proposals for educational accountability criticize the assumption that school inputs and resources can serve as a reliable index of either the quality or the value of school programs. They argue that greater emphasis should be placed on results, meaning student learning and performance. With certain conditions to be outlined we agree with this position, and it is supported by research. In the much-discussed Coleman report,[1] standardized achievement tests designed to measure student skills in reading, writing and computation were administered to approximately 650,000 students in more than 4,000 schools across the country. On all of the tests given, minority students of either Indian, Puerto Rican, Black or Mexican-American descent scored significantly lower than whites. These results and others which have followed support the argument that many minority children experience lower school achievement than is generally true for white children, especially in comparison to whites from more favored socio-economic backgrounds.

The theory has been commonly accepted that differences in school achievement can be largely accounted for by differences in school inputs, i.e., by such factors as the teacher, plant facilities, size of the library and so forth. Yet Coleman found wide disparities in achievement even though schools for minority children do not, on average, function in older, more crowded or less adequate buildings, or have significantly larger classes or less adequate textbooks. The belief that wide categorical differences exist between resources available to minority and white children holds only to a limited extent, for it is founded largely on comparisons between northern ghetto schools and more affluent suburban systems, where disparities in school resources are a harsh reality. But as Jencks has observed, such comparisons overlook the fact that many whites live in smaller and often poorer communities where schools frequently leave as much to be desired as those found in larger city ghettos.[2]

Furthermore, children with similar backgrounds from each of these groups did not perform appreciably better in systems that had modern plant facilities, larger libraries and higher per-pupil expenditures than comparably grouped children in systems with poorer facilities, smaller libraries and lower expenditures. In other words, the direct relationship between school achievement and educational resources which Coleman expected to find simply did not occur.

But though we are in agreement that school resources and inputs cannot serve as an exclusive measure of the value of school programs or the ultimate effectiveness on the school in promoting student learning, it is at this juncture that we dissent from other assumptions underlying proposals for teacher accountability. They are correct in calling attention to results, but when student performance is disappointing and falls short of what we believe it ought to be, what remedy do these proposals offer? More often than not they shift attention to another input factor—the classroom teacher. To the extent that these proposals ignore the responsibilities and actions of students, their parents, school administrators, school committees and the general community, they imply that teachers are an exclusive influence in determining what students will learn, how they will perform and eventually in what they achieve. Not only is this assumption superficial and out of touch with reality, it presents a major obstacle to the improvement of student performance and to the achievement of many outcomes that are important in education.

In commenting on the Coleman study, Silberman noted:

> This finding has been interpreted as meaning the schools have no effect on student learning. It means nothing of the sort. This evidence suggests only that the schools are remarkably uniform in their effects on student learning. Differences in student achievements from school to school seem to be due more to differences in the student's own family background and in the backgrounds of their fellow students than to differences in the quality of the schools themselves.[3]

Consequently, an important conclusion of the study was that "schools bring little to bear on a child's achievement that is independent of his background and social context; and that this very lack of an independent effect means that the inequalities imposed on children by their home, neighborhood, and peer environment are carried along to become the inequalities with which they confront adult life at the end of schooling."[4] It is crucial to note that the conclusion is not that schools bring little to bear on a child's achievement, but that they bring little to bear which is *independent* of such factors. Some minority children overcome rather severe limitations, eventually succeeding in school and over the post-school years, but presently they are the exception, not the rule. If most of these children are to succeed, then these factors, which seem to have such an important bearing on school performance, must be understood and altered, for they represent a debilitating influence on children and from the outset seriously compromise the benefits that they might otherwise derive from their schooling.

By no means do the findings from these studies indicate that schools and teachers should be indifferent to student failure or that they are doing all they possibly can to prevent it. Schools should represent a liberating force in a child's life and whenever possible present students with opportunities for becoming something other than what their circumstances would have ordinarily limited them to be. Admittedly, some schools fail in this effort, while others may even inhibit the development of dispositions and abilities that should be of concern to a school. But this research does not support the contention that this is generally the case, let alone that it accounts for the incidence of failure often cited as a justification for accountability demands. What it does reveal is that the influences on a child's mind and personality have complex origins and include his or her family, peers, neighborhood, the media, and a thousand and one personal experiences, the relative influences of which are only beginning to be appreciated and have never been codified with anything approaching the accuracy that is possible in factoring elements of a manufactured product. If we are to understand school failure, we must understand the full context in which it occurs, however complex and difficult the task may be. Accountability procedures which hold teachers solely responsible for student failure short-circuit this understanding, for they rest on the questionable assumptions that teachers are its primary cause or have it within their power to control whatever is. Both assumptions are doubtful and raise logical as well as moral problems where teacher accountability is concerned. The logical problem is essentially one of practicality. If, as proponents of accountability have argued, a fundamental justification for this concept is that it will provide the means by which undesirable student performance can be remedied, how can this be done by procedures which place primary emphasis on only one of its possible causes—a factor which research suggests may be less significant than other factors they ignore?

There has been some attempt to avoid this practical limitation through the "value-added" concept. In this proposal a teacher or contractor would not be expected to reach a common level of achievement with all students, but would be rewarded for advancing achievement or the value he adds to a child's learning from a given point; e.g., he would not be expected to have students enrolled in a fifth-grade class all read at that level or beyond by the end their fifth year. Instead, students would be pre-tested and their expected achievement determined on an individual basis. Under the value-added approach, if a child reads at a second-grade level by the time he reaches the fifth grade, not only would one presume that certain reading difficulties exist requiring special attention, but one would expect an advancement from *that* level, one that is reasonable to expect within the available time period.

This procedure establishes more reasonable expectations for both students and teachers and would likely prove beneficial as a regular practice. But it is doubtful that it should be erected into a system of accountability under performance contracting—first, because of the criticisms already noted, and second, because under the present structure of American education one may seriously question how much professional influence teachers really have within the school. To what degree do they govern its practices, establish budgetary priorities, influence what will or will not be included within curricula, participate in significant decisions—in a word, have control over the very means through which they must work to influence student performance? Moreover, if teachers do not have this control, do they have access to those who do, such as administrators and school board members, and how is their position or status in these relationships viewed, as that of professionals or strictly employees?

Parents influence the attitudes their sons and daughters bring to school; they can be supportive in their comments about learning, the work of teachers and the value of education, or they can deride and be constantly critical of all of these things. The most common derision is that teachers are underworked, overpaid and "have all of that vacation time." If stated often enough, these comments and the adult opinions they reflect will influence a student's attitude toward learning. How accessible or available are parents in regard to their children's education? Or for that matter, how accessible are legislators, taxpayers and others who influence the amount of resources available to schools, and to what extent is the professional work of teachers assisted or impeded by these groups? For example, if teachers believe an additional reading instructor or counselor, better textbooks, special materials or a vocational work-study program will help their students, and the school board or taxpayers refuse to provide the necessary funding, to what extent are teachers then causally responsible for student performance? From the standpoint of having a direct influence on student competency, to what degree are teachers responsible when confronted daily by students who are disruptive or inattentive in class because of drug- or alcohol-related problems? What if these problems occur in a community that refuses to admit that they exist or repeatedly ignores requests for programs to help students cope with the difficulties they are facing? Under these circumstances what are teachers to do, assuming of course that learning requires some degree of attention and that often before a student can or will give it, other priorities and problems in life must be addressed?

In ethical theory, the concepts of *ought* and *should* carry the implication of possibility. The notion that "ought" implies "can" simply means that from a practical as well as a logical standpoint there would be little point in telling someone that he ought to do something or that he is expected to perform in a certain manner if either is beyond the realm of possibility. The point was raised whether it would be ethically justifiable to hold an agent accountable for matters resulting from the actions of others; this consideration is especially important in situations where the control of conditions enabling or preventing a person from satisfying an expected performance rest largely in the hands of others. We agree with Coleman's conclusions: Schools are important, but they are by no means an exclusive factor in the matter of student attitudes and achievement. How much do these other groups influence student performance, and if accountability is to be the answer, what approach should be taken, recognizing that from a causal standpoint there are many influences on learning and that responsibility for it must be shared?

In one community, which shall remain anonymous, the funding for schools has reached a level where operating budgets can no longer support programs in art, music, or athletics. Several writers acknowledge that numerous groups influence what happens to children in school, and some have even suggested that as a consequence all should be accountable if any are to be. But beyond this recognition little is offered in the way of description or proposals as to the form this accountability should assume, and however important it may be, its practicality appears remote for several reasons, most of which have to do with the history of education and the manner in which authority and governance structures have evolved within school systems and in their relationships to the public. Taxpayers elect school committee members, and there is a sense in which the latter are held accountable at election time, but if the taxpayers who put them in office become disgruntled over taxes and refuse to vote the funding necessary to support school programs, to whom are these taxpayers accountable? The preceding questions bring us to another, closely related issue.

Entitlement, school governance and the issue of agent expectations

We have argued that the influences on any given level of student achievement are usually quite varied in their origin and that it is simple-minded to contend that any single factor can account for learning in a causal sense. The factors which impinge on student learning are complex and, like it or not, this condition must be recognized. But this does not mean that teachers are absolved of responsibility for the learning of their students either causally, in the decisions and actions they take, or expectationally, in what may be reasonably expected of them because of their professional role. Teachers have numerous responsibilities which fit into both of these categories and in relation to which they should be accountable.

Teachers have a professional responsibility to maintain an environment and processes that contribute to the learning and development of their students. Despite the fact that their work is conditioned by the influence and sometimes the constraints imposed by others, we expect that they will do whatever they can to meet this general responsibility. There also is the closely related expectation that they be competent in handling the various tasks that must be completed in carrying out this mission and that they be competent in fulfilling many other responsibilities associated with their professional role. Teachers should be expected to acquire and to maintain a sufficient understanding of children, learning, methods of teaching and their academic interests to be able to bring to their teaching the best that the state of the art and their present circumstances will allow. Moreover, from a causal reference, in their daily work teachers make many decisions and take numerous actions for which they are directly responsible, decisions and actions which tend toward the satisfaction or nonfulfillment of these expectations. They should be accountable for the responsibilities one would normally associate with their position, and also for the actions they take or fail to take in the process of meeting them.

The principle difficulties, of course, are understanding the nature of these responsibilities and how to develop procedures for accountability that are appropriate in relation to them as well as the profession they serve. The challenge presented can be appreciated if we consider one or two accountability demands and the difficult questions of school governance and entitlement that are associated with them. Presumably, parents have an obligation to provide for the welfare of their children and a clear interest in any matters affecting it. If there is a group entitled to some form of educational accountability, it would seem that they are. But to what are they entitled? To recall a former example, suppose a teacher introduces a book which she believes is in the interests of her students to read, but a parent disapproves in the belief that some of the book's content is morally objectionable. At this level, if the parent is sincere, there is a sense in which she would be negligent in her responsibility as a parent not to inquire about its use. Although she may not be well informed about such matters, it seems reasonable to maintain that where there is suspicion that something may be wrong for her children, she does have an obligation and a basic right to inquire. There are, then, at least moral grounds to support her entitlement to some kind of explanation concerning this matter and a *prima facie* obligation on the teacher's part to give it, especially if she is primarily responsible for the book's selection and use.

But let us suppose further that the teacher offers an explanation outlining the book's literary merits and why she believes it appropriate for the students she is teaching, yet the parent remains unconvinced, demanding that the book be removed from the classroom. Should her entitlement under accountability extend to making such a demand and having it satisfied? The matter is not as simple as contending that the parent's demand should not be construed as accountability but only as a request for the book's removal. This is so, first, because the issue essentially concerns what should be considered a justifiable expectation under entitlement in a relationship where the teacher has taken steps to offer an account of her reasons for using the book. In this relationship the parent believes that her request to have the book removed from the classroom is justified and that her expectation should be satisfied. Second, while it is true that the teacher has already been accountable to the extent of having provided an explanation of her reasons, it is clear the matter could be carried further, e.g., the parent might state that she expects the book to be withdrawn, that if it is not she will go to the superintendent and school committee requesting the teacher's removal as well and will organize other, similarly minded parents for this purpose. In essence, if her demand is not satisfied the parent intends to implement procedures to make the teacher answerable under a more extreme form of accountability.

This case is not unique. A similar problem occurred in Drake, North Dakota, where a teacher was not rehired because he had used Kurt Vonnegut's *Slaughterhouse Five,* in a high school English class. All copies of this book were removed from the school and burned, and several other books in use were simply withdrawn from the curriculum.[5] It is historical fact that teachers, school administrators and several school board members in Kanawha County, West Virginia, were embroiled in an open and sometimes violent conflict with parents over a textbook series which a number of parents considered immoral and unpatriotic. Warrants were issued to the superintendent and four board members at the request of one of the parents, charging that they had contributed to the delinquency of minors.[6]

Conflicts over books, discussion topics and units of study are not always as dramatic as the famous Scopes Trial or the examples presented; nevertheless, more than one teacher has been dismissed in circumstances of this kind. Certainly, a fundamental problem is how to maintain the right of parents to inquire about their childrens' education and have justifiable expectations satisfied, and yet maintain a climate in which educators can carry out their work professionally. The parent in our example has every right to inquire about the book's use, and under the circumstances is entitled to an explanation. We might even agree that she has a further right to refuse to have her child read it but this is not her intention in this situation. She is demanding that the book be removed from the classroom, thereby denying others access to it. The distinction between demands which effect only the children of petitioning parents and those which effect other children is important. Compliance with the demand in this case infringes on the right of other parents to have their children experience material which they and the teacher believe is beneficial. Though a teacher's obligations would include the obligation to account when justified, what began as a legitimate accountability expectation—that is, to have the book's use in the curriculum explained—moved to the status of an expectation conflicting with another professional obligation of the teacher: her obligation to provide what she believes is educationally worthwhile and in the best interests of other students. She may be quite aware that a number of students in her class intend to go to college and will encounter professors who expect students to be familiar with the literature she has selected. What are her responsibilities under these circumstances? To some the answer is simple: If she is smart and wants to keep her position, she should give in, but where does this leave her students and the expectations they will face upon entering college?

The matter of entitlement is even more complicated if we consider the question of how much discretion parents should have concerning the education of their children? Should parents be permitted to prohibit their children from studying black history or any social issues or part of history that may happen to challenge their values? Freedom in this regard is not entirely unconditional, e.g., though parents may choose alternative means of schooling, choose they must, for in many states until a child reaches a certain age school attendance in one form or another is mandatory, and in most cases children are required by law to satisfy minimum requirements in math, history and English. School integration by court order offers another example of limitations on parental choice in educational matters. There are no doubt various reasons why we have compulsory school attendance and some may have to do with entrance into the labor market and certain vocations, but ostensibly it is out of recognition that children too have rights, and though they may be under the guardship of their parents, these early years are formative and it is during them that children must acquire the understandings, skills and attitudes that will suit them for a life which must go on long after they have left their parents; a life that will have implications for other members of society.

Parenthood does not imply ownership, and it is a fact that not all parents act in the best interests of their children. Through neglect, abuse, indifference or ignorance, they may well set patterns and limitations with which a child and others in society will have to contend for many years. It is partly for these reasons that the fulfillment of expectations under accountability must be restricted to what is reasonable and justified. True, the status of being a parent does obligate one to try to do what is in the best interests of a child, but we must recognize that teachers have a similar obligation professionally. If the question becomes, to whom are their primary obligations due? the answer must be: to children and to what the principles of their profession require. Involved then, is not only the matter of expectations, but how determination of their reasonableness and justification should be procedurally handled. People have a right to hold differing expectations, justified or not, to voice their demands and to register complaints; but the real problem is whether the prerogatives of entitlement assumed in current conceptions of accountability would permit these differences to be resolved fairly, giving sufficient recognition not only to the obligations of all parties concerned, but to the needs of a profession if its responsibilities are to be met.

From the standpoint of accountability, student achievement and progress have been reported through written reports and personal conferences over the years; parents have had the right to question and voice differences with teachers and school administrators, and to petition school board members; periodic reports are given to the public concerning school budgets, fiscal allocations and needs; citizens have the right to vote on school expenditures, to select and remove school board members, who, in turn, have a similar prerogative concerning school personnel.

If the structure is inadequate from the standpoint of accountability, the reasons should be explored, but we doubt that it can be improved by setting up accountability arrangements which ignore general presumptions usually held in regard to most professions. A parent has every right to ask about the reasons which underlie a diagnosis and treatment of his child's illness, but it in not generally presumed that he should dictate to the physician what that treatment should be, let alone tell him how to treat the children of other parents.

Taxpayers are entitled to an accounting of how their money is spent, but once the decision has been made to fund the construction of a highway, their entitlement does not extend to setting the specifications for its bridges or directing its construction, and a similar understanding usually exists whenever an electrician, plumber or technician is asked to make a repair.

Professional accountability: selecting appropriate forms and methods of accounting

From the standpoint of accountability, the foregoing issues involving responsibility and entitlement are important, but they lead to a more fundamental issue concerning our view of teaching as a profession and whether or not there are approaches to accountability that would be more suitable in serving the purposes of its mission. It has been suggested that teaching is not really a profession because those who practice it lack perspective on what they do, and that it is precisely because of this and the fact that conditions similar to the following now occur that greater accountability is needed:

> By and large, teachers, principals, and superintendents are decent, intelligent, and caring people who try to do their best by their lights. If they make

a botch of it, and an uncomfortably large number do, it is because it simply never occurs to more than a handful to ask *why* they are doing what they are doing—to think seriously or deeply about the purposes or consequences of education. This mindlessness—the failure or refusal to think seriously about educational purpose, the reluctance to question established practice—is not the monopoly of the public school; it is diffused remarkably evenly throughout the entire educational system, and indeed the entire society.[7]

There are several remarks that need to be made about the foregoing. The first is that whether or not teaching is a profession, goals in education must still be chosen and have a setting in which they can be effectively pursued. Can this really be done under interpretations of accountability similar to the following?

> Public education is not our special birthright. Rather, it is a tax-supported service in which teachers participate. Public education belongs to all the people, and all the people have the right to seek its improvement, to determine its purposes, and to evaluate its outcomes.[8]

If accountability "to the people" is taken to imply a situation in which all the people may determine goals, choose materials and evaluate educational outcomes, this concept will continue to be unmanageable. Not only do various conceptions of accountability exist, but there is little agreement within the constituencies holding them as to what the goals of education should be, much less any consensus on the standards that should be employed in their evaluation. There is no such thing as "the people," but only groups of people, representing all walks of life, dissimilar in their values, interests, beliefs and expectations. Sincere efforts should be made to hear their views and, more importantly, when they have a primary influence on education, an effort should be made to inform them about educational concerns and issues; but to incorporate this diversity in the daily operation of schools would be impractical, could very well be disastrous from the standpoint of teaching, and reveals a basic insensitivity to the problems generated when entitlement is too broadly interpreted. There are few other professions in which the professional is as subject to nonprofessional opinions and constraints concerning what may or may not be done in his work as the public school teacher. If teaching is not a profession, perhaps this is because it is not encouraged or allowed to be practiced as one.[9]

Second, if teaching is not a profession, a lack of perspective on the part of teachers may partially explain it, but it also may have something to do with the perspectives of school administrators and the outside groups already mentioned. Administrators also have professional responsibilities. Generally speaking, school principals have considerable authority in relation to school philosophy, students, teachers, curricula, and the enforcement of rules and regulations. Their outlooks and beliefs and the manner in which they exercise their authority can have a profound influence on the climate of a school, on the ways in which it conducts its affairs and on the quality of the human relationships that are a part of its life. They can be authoritarian in outlook or essentially democratic in their approach to issues, provide leadership that fosters a collegial and supportive atmosphere in relation to the work of teachers and students or be essentially out of touch with their concerns. The activities of teaching and learning involve an enterprise in which there are bound to be many issues and points of view, and it is an enterprise that is sufficiently complex to encounter innumerable problems in the process of carrying it out. The real question is whether relationships in education can be approached and structured to incorporate forms of communication, inquiry, interest and accountability that have the effect of promoting a better understanding of what this enterprise involves, a better recognition of goals and aims that are worthwhile in the education of children, and a clearer understanding of what is necessary in terms of resources and commitment if they are to be achieved.

The view that education is conducted in an atmosphere of mindlessness cannot be due to a common belief that having an education is unimportant, since schooling is something we say should be extended to all and have already provided for many. Of course, it may be encouraged by attitudes toward education which do see it as an industrial process, as something necessary to go through and endure but only as a means to something else, the ultimate value being perceived not in the experience of learning and the personal qualities of mind and character to which it should lead, but instead in what it will bring—a better job, more earnings, success. The problem is not that these things are unimportant or that they are not needed in the lives of people, but that in a climate of valuing an education only for what it will do and not for what it is, much can be lost in the way of appreciation for its intrinsic value. A situation is created in which schooling and those who carry it on come to have something less then an exalted status because they too are viewed as a means, as part of a process the whole value and purpose of which have been made to rest on extrinsic rewards which may or may not be realized.

In the first part of this study it was observed that there are various ways of accounting and being answerable for one's responsibilities. Some were stated to be negative due to their imposition of penalties, while others were quite different in their potential to yield a better understanding of responsibilities, as well as the decisions, actions and reasoning associated with them. A teacher who engages in actions contrary to his professional responsibilities should be required to explain his reasons for doing so, and if his neglect of responsibility persists and is sufficiently severe, it may be justifiable to hold him accountable under some form of penalty. The various forms of accountability we have discussed are appropriate and do feature in the structure of education. But we should be concerned with the relative emphasis these forms of accounting now receive, and which among them are most consistent with educational purposes and will tend to offset the mindlessness Silberman describes.

We offer a final example to illustrate this point, and in doing so return to the hypothetical argument presented earlier. The main features of performance contracting do include establishing performance objectives, teaching, reporting student progress and accordingly assigning or with-holding rewards. But after going through these activities, what are contractors to do when they encounter student failure? Or are we to assume that under this form of accountability the problem of student failure will disappear? We find this implausible for reasons already given: The problem of student failure is a function of many factors and influences that are more complex than this approach to accountability assumes. True, reporting student progress is a suitable and legitimate form of accounting on those occasions when there is a need to have information on how well students have done in relation to certain aims, and it is true that positive forms of reinforcement can be effective in motivating people. But taken alone or even together, neither form of accountability can yield the reasons "why" students fail. If teachers do not think seriously about the aims of education and the reasons for student failure, or are reluctant to question established practice, it may be that doing so is discouraged by a system of accountability which is already too restrictive, one which tends to reward for not asking "why." Or it may be because the fruits of questioning and creative thinking are sometimes expressed but seldom come to any significant consequence. If Silberman's impression is correct, then education cannot be improved by conceptions of accountability which foster these conditions.

From a different perspective, accountability relationships in education might be more productive if greater emphasis were placed on the rational forms of accounting we have identified, that is, on those which involve analysis and the activities of justifying and explaining, forms of account-ing that promote questioning and a better understanding of educational problems and issues because by their nature they have the potential to yield deeper insight.

In addition, professional accountability relationships ought to be more reciprocal and involve these rational forms of accounting not only within the school but in relation to the primary and external groups that have an influence on the quality of education. Historically, the governance and authority structures in education have been hierarchical, meaning that students are usually accountable to teachers and the administration, teachers to department chairs and their principal, the principal to the superintendent, and the superintendent to the school committee. It is not our position that this hierarchical structure should be altered, although there may be some reasons for doing so, but that it should be more collegial and rationally focused. In maintaining that these relationships ought to be reciprocal, we mean that they should involve mutual exchange where the activities of explaining and justifying operate in both directions. When school committees, superintendents and school administrators implement policies or actions that significantly affect the conditions in which teachers and students must do their work, they should provide an accounting of their reasons for doing so, and prior to reaching final decisions provide opportunities for discussion and the expression of points of view on the part of those affected.

Several characteristics have been identified with rational and democratic forms of procedure and social organization. Two considerations support our position that improvement in student learning will not occur unless the value of these characteristics is recognized and they become incorporated in relationships involving educational accountability. On the one hand, many problems in education today are complex. Their solution will require knowledge from many disciplines, the efforts of numerous groups and the best in thinking and commitment that capable and conscientious people have to offer. If we are to deal with the problem of school failure, we must understand "why" it occurs and acknowledge those things that can and cannot be remedied by the school alone. Furthermore, if change is required for the improvement of learning and student performance, then those who have a primary influence on their outcome must have sufficient understanding to recognize the need for change and sufficient flexibility and commitment to implement it.

Second, adult responsibilities for children are of the highest order; they concern human lives, the ultimate directions of which are bound to be influenced to a major degree by the manner in which these responsibilities are viewed and carried out. If it is a primary purpose of education to develop a questioning attitude in children, the dispositions of reasonableness, critical thinking and moral sensitivity, how effectively can these goals be promoted if these same qualities are not respected or encouraged in those who teach them? The strongest argument for implementing more rational forms of accountability in education rests on their consistency with its aims and the simple fact that education cannot be improved nor can these aims be fully realized without them. In our opinion, effective accountability relationships can be achieved along these lines, but they will only occur if those who influence education at all levels recognize their importance.

CHAPTER 8

Summary and conclusions

The elements and principles of accountability

Examination of several concepts in this study indicated that it would be in the interest of greater clarity if a sharper distinction were drawn between the normative and theoretical aspects of accountability. Considerations relevant to the first concern the grounds supporting an obligation to account, whether the circumstances in which it is to be given are fair, and the influence that personal values and moral orientation can have on the matter of compliance. Our analysis established that *prima facie* obligations are incurred when an agent is responsible, either casually or expectationally, for acts, performances or matters in relation to which others have a valid interest, by virtue of the fact that such acts or matters have a significant bearing on their lives and that because of this consideration various moral and/or legal institutions support their entitlement to some form of accounting and at least a *prima facie* obligation to provide it.

The notion of a "valid responsibility" would imply, casually, acts or performances committed, influenced or omitted by the agent; and, expectationally, those acts or performances which are consistent with the roles from which they are said to derive, possible to satisfy and not unjustified by other considerations that may have equal or greater validity with respect to their assignment, satisfaction or expectation. Granting these conditions, it is clear from the examples already presented that *prima facie* obligations can be altered by further considerations.

Whether or not an *overall* obligation exists could be partially contingent on whether the purposes of the relationship and form of accountability expected adversely effect or seriously compromise other responsibilities of the accountant. Since this concept also implies the potential of being answerable in a manner prejudicial to the interests of an accountant, fairness would seem to require that within reason the various standards and procedures used in the process of appraising an agent's performance be mutually understood, consistent and reliable.

The preceding conditions are relevant to the normative problem of whether or not an agent should be accountable in any given situation and whether or not the expectation or demand for accountability is justified. However, within accountability situations the question Does accountability exist? differs in the sense that it involves a mix of theoretical considerations as well—for example, the relative influence which any number of factors may potentially have on the degree of actual or probable compliance associated with the relationship. These would include a person's moral orientation, but in addition various circumstantial factors attending particular occasions of accountability. We contend that these circumstantial factors conjoin the moral posture of people in determining the responses they will make to the moral and legal obligations they incur, including those involving their accountability. Finally, the degree to which accountability exists in any relationship will involve whether or not the form of accounting selected and the manner in which the agent is expected to be accountable are really suitable for the purposes accountability is to serve.

We argued that moral accountability and more rational forms of accounting are to be preferred where they are required and workable. A presumption exists in favor of moral accountability because of the greater freedom and personal autonomy it allows, but because people are not similarly disposed in their response to moral obligations, the need for legal accountability and the additional compliance motivation it involves also must be recognized. Furthermore, there are many occasions of accountability where simply relating facts and events is all that is needed. But it is one thing to report that certain events have occurred and quite a different matter to explain or to justify "why" they occurred. It is for this reason that rational forms of accounting must be employed and have value in relation to matters where they are needed, for they have the potential to yield this additional insight.

Degree of accountability: final analysis

Our former model depicting the strength of an accountability relationship has been modified to include these factors in figure 8.1. In effect, the requirements which various forms of accounting impose have been augmented by their suitability for the relationship and by the added factor of compliance. The influence of both factors should not be underestimated or oversimplified. It is our position that in arrangements involving a high degree of compliance and suitability, a change in either would tend to produce a corresponding increase or decrease in the degree of accountability operating, the dependent variable being represented by projected intersections of the XY axis. In other words, at these levels if probability of compliance increases or the accounting form becomes more suitable, the relationship is strengthened, whereas a decrease in either would tend to diminish or weaken it. Because of the above, it is tempting to assume that the influence of each of these variables is indifferent; that a loss of influence of either can be adequately compensated by an opposite change in the other. If this assumption were valid,

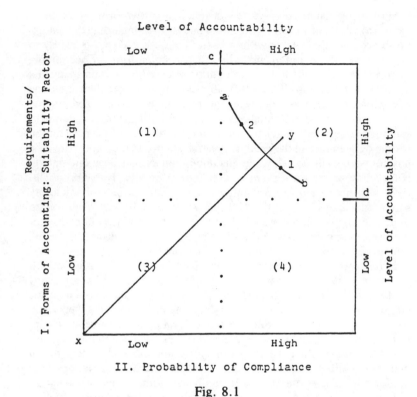

Fig. 8.1

the degree of accountability operating in the relationship could be maintained at any point on the a b curve in figure 8.1. Though point 1 might represent a less desirable form of accounting, it is offset by a higher probability of compliance. Similarly, at point 2, the diminished compliance factor is balanced by a more suitable form of accounting. In essence, this interpretation would hold that the relationship depicted in figure 8.1 is indifferent with respect to the overall accountability achieved so long as any point on line AB represents a point of mutual compensation. This interpretation would be correct in those cases where, at the outset, compliance and suitability are high, since minor changes in either would probably not be that significant because some manner of compensation could be made. Unfortunately, this interpretation does not hold under all conditions, and it is questionable whether this kind of compensation could be achieved when they occur.

On the one hand, compliance is a function of two primary determinants: (a) the agent's overall perception and attitude regarding the obligatio to account, that is, his willingness to comply; and (b) his ability to do so under the requirements which a particular form of accounting imposes. When (1) the form of accounting selected, is beyond an agent's ability to satisfy, it is obvious that (2) probability of compliance will be negligible, however willing the agent might happen to be. The point is that any improvement in suitability of the accounting form will compensate for a compliance deficiency only where it has been a primary reason for the deficiency and the agent is generally willing to comply; or, if he has not been so disposed, where his unwillingness has been due only to his recognition that the form of accounting was previously inappropriate.

On the other hand, it is doubtful that a significant lack of suitability can be adequately compensated by changes in compliance. When a form of accounting is inappropriate in terms of what it requires of an agent or the basic purposes for which accountability was established, it would remain so irrespective of the agent's intention.

In other words, though factors 1 and 2 influence level of accountability, what is questionable is the ability of either to remedy a deficiency in the other, especially if it is severe. There is, then, a point in the continuum of both variables below which any change in the other would be ineffective as far as making accountability a more viable relationship. In figure 8.1 this point is theoretical and represented below intersections c and d, where either the probability of compliance is so low that it makes little difference how suitable the form of accounting is, or where the form is so inappropriate that compliance would be inconsequential.

In essence, if the degree of accountability is to be relatively high in such relationships, a fairly stable equilibrium must be maintained between variables 1 and 2. It is our interpretation that the highest levels of accountability will occur in those relationships best described by quadrant 2, where probability of compliance is high and the form of accounting selected is suitable to the arrangement. Quadrants 1 and 4 would include cases where the degree of accountability is diminished by either a low compliance factor or an inappropriate form of accounting. Section 3 would be descriptive of any relationship in which the form of accounting is unsuitable for the reasons stated and the likelihood of compliance is for all practical purposes nonexistent.

Accountability relationships are pervasive throughout all levels of society and involve individuals, groups and institutions in practically all areas of human activity. For this reason it would be impossible within the scope of this writing to provide specific answers that would be suitable for every relationship where accountability is an issue, and it has not been our intention to do so. But our analysis has identified several elements and conditions which are essential to a conceptual understanding of accountability, and it has revealed a number of considerations and principles that ought to guide practical applications of this concept. For example, various forms of accounting, responsibility, obligation and entitlement will always be involved in accountability relationships, whether the relationships in question happen to concern the law and criminal justice, education, medicine, business, consumer affairs, politics, or even our family and friends. We contend that the way in which these elements and principles are interpreted and actually obtain in specific situations will largely determine the degree of accountability operating on those occasions, and also will affect the overall quality and effectiveness of the relationships they involve.

In one form or another accountability is a reality in almost everyone's life. Consequently, we believe the issues and questions raised throughout this discussion warrant further study and should prove interesting to those who pursue them.

Notes

1 Accounting to others and being answerable

1 C. T. Onions, ed., *The Oxford Universal Dictionary on Historical Principles* (Oxford University Press, 1955), p. 12.
2 It is alleged that the term *accountable* was formed on the verb *account* and introduced around 1583. This is open to some question, since the most likely root connotation of *account* meaning "to answer for" or "to explain" did not come into use until 1679. If correct, the derivation of *accountable* must be either from the original, now obsolete usage "to count, reckon, or calculate," or from the use of *account* as a substantive. The latter seems the more plausible explanation, since the substantive form of *account* implying "a statement as to responsibilities generally and answering for conduct," was common during the Middle English period and therefore meets the obvious requirements of having been antecedent to the term *accountable* and similar in implication.
3 *Webster's Seventh New Collegiate Dictionary* (Springfield, Mass.: Merriam, 1965), p. 6; *Webster's Ninth New Collegiate Dictionary* (Springfield, Mass.: Merriam, 1987), p. 50.
4 Ludwig Wittgenstein, *Philosophical Investigations* trans. by G. E. M. Anscombe (New York: Macmillan, 1968), p. 32e
5 As we shall see, these forms of accounting by no means exhaust the terms implication.
6 The initial account concerning x, y and z is more or less adequate to the extent that it corresponds to what actually occurred. In the second case the scientist has gone beyond merely reporting an observation of phenomena and, by reference to his knowledge of certain principles and laws, advanced what is essentially a hypothesis concerning their nature. Of course, the original account and the observations which it attempts to summarize could be questioned. But what would be in question is whether the scientist actually observed what he claims to have observed. Confirmation of his claim would require either reexamining the phenomena or appealing to other observers; it is here assumed that phenomena are given and are more or less equally accessible to persons having similar characteristics and dispositions to observe, observing under similar conditions.
7 Similarly, having to disclose the contents, ingredients or composition of various products is a form of accountability, but it seems less complex in

terms of the requirements which must be satisfied than having to explain or justify their use.

8 Lessinger and Tyler, *Accountability in Education* (Worthington: Charles A. Jones, 1971) p. 1; Terrel H. Bell, "Educational Accountability Starts at the Top," Frank J.. Sciara and Richard J. Jantz eds., *Accountability in American Education* (Boston: Allyn and Bacon, 1972), pp. 152–158

9 Terrel H. Bell, "The New Look at Federal Aid to Education," speech to the Michigan Association of School Boards (Grand Rapids, Sept. 24, 1970), in Sciara and Jantz, *Accountability in American Education*, pp. 41–47

10 Leon Lessinger, *Every Kid a Winner: Accountability in Education* (New York: Simon and Schuster, 1970), p. 3.

11 Lessinger and Tyler, *Accountability in Education*, p. 2.

12 Ibid, p. 30.

13 "Cost of Education Index: 1971–72," *School Management* 16 (Jan. 1972, pp. 21–57; James G. Albert, "Wanted: Experiment in Reducing the Cost of Education." *Phi Delta Kappan* 55, no. 7 (March 1974), pp. 444–445

14 William M. Cruickshank, "The Development of Education for Exceptional Children," in William M. Cruickshank and G. Orville Johnson, eds., *Education of Exceptional Children and Youth* (Englewood Cliffs: Prentice Hall, 1967), pp. 3–44.

15 William Proxmire, *Report From Wasteland: America's Military-Industrial Complex* (New York: Praeger, 1970), pp. 1–65.

16 Some would argue that people vote by the purchases they make. This is true to a degree, but in some respects the argument is specious. The safety features incorporated in the Tucker automobile were never available to the general public. To many people a car is a necessity. Their purchases must be made from automobiles that are available within the range they can afford, even though no automobiles within this group incorporate features they may desire.

17 During this period it was estimated that three hundred infant deaths and six thousand serious injuries occur each year due to flammable clothing material. See the *New York Times*. July 28, 1973, p. 8.

2 Accountability and the aims of education

1 Lessinger, *Every Kid a Winner*, p. 67.

2 James A. Mecklenburger and John A. Wilson, "Learning C. O. D.: Can the Schools Buy Success?" *Saturday Review*, Sept. 18, 1971, pp. 62–65, 76–79.

3 Ibid.

4 Edmund L. Pincoffs, "Educational Accountability," *Studies in Philosophy and Education* 8 (Fall 1973), p. 136.

5 Ibid., pp. 136–137.

6 Ibid., p. 138.

7 Ibid.

8   Ibid., pp. 138–139.
9   Ibid.,pp. 141–142.
10 Ibid., p. 143.
11 Neil Postman and Charles Weingartner, *Teaching as a Subversive Activity* New York: Delacorte Press, 19669), pp. 1–15.
12 Postman and Weingertner, *Teaching*, 15.
13 Charles E. Silberman, *Crisis in the Classroom*(New York: Vintage, 1971), pp. 8–9.
14 Richard S. Peters, *Ethics and Education* (Atlanta: Scott, Foresman, 1967), pp. 49–54.
15 Ibid.
16 R. M. Hare, *Freedom and Reason* (New York: Oxford University Press, 1965), pp. 1–2.
17 Ibid., pp. 1–2.
18 William Frankena, *Ethics* (Englewood Cliffs: Prentice-Hall, 1963), pp. 5–6.
19 See Peters's chapter "Freedom" in *Ethics in Education*, pp. 103–115.
20 Israel Scheffler, "Moral Education and the Democratic Ideal," in *Reason and Teaching* (New York: Bobbs-Merrill, 1973), pp. 136–145.
21 Scheffler, *Reason and Teaching*, pp. 142–143.
22 Lessinger, *Every Kid a Winner*, p. 10.
23 Peters, *Ethics and Education*, p. 9.
24 Lessinger, *Every Kid a Winner*, p. 10
25 Ibid.
26 James Mecklenburger and John Wilson, "The Performance Contract in Gary," *Phi Delta Kappan* 52 (March 1971), pp. 406–411
27 Girard D. Hottleman, "Performance Contracting is a Hoax!: in *Sciara and Jantz, Accountability in American Education*, pp. 266–267.
28 Ibid., p. 265.
29 Ibid. This statement is quoted by Hottleman and appears in "Freedom, Bureaucracy, and Schooling," *A. S. C. D. Yearbook* (Washington, D. C. *NEA*, 1971).
30 Lawrence Kohlberg, with Phillip Whitten, "Understanding the Hidden Curriculum," *Annual Editions: Readings in Education* (Guilford, Conn: Dushkin Publishing Group, 1973), p. 205.

3 The basis for accountability relationships

1   This position was taken, in part, from "The Principles of Justice," in John Rawls, *A Theory of Justice* (Cambridge: Harvard University Press, 1971), pp. 54–117.
2   *The Republic of Plato,* trans. Francis M. Cornford (Oxford: Oxford University Press, 1965), p. 7.
3   W. D. Ross, *The Right and the Good* (Oxford: Clarendon Press, 1930), p. 19.

4 Richard B. Brandt, *Ethical Theory* (Englewood Cliffs: Prentice-Hall, 1959), pp. 367–368.

5 It could also be argued that one generation has responsibilities to those younger or yet unborn. I have in mind here the cross-generational responsibility to conserve resources, protect an environment that will one day pass to others, and provide systems of educational opportunity either commensurate with or substantially better than those enjoyed by the generation in question. However important these responsibilities may seem, historically it would be stretching the point to say that any generation has been accountable concerning its performance in their regard.

6 An instance of (a) is illustrated by the following *prima facie* obligation: If X promises Y that he will do *z*, in the absence of any relevant factor qualification, X is morally obligated to do *z*. Under normal circumstances, if the promissory arrangement between X and Y involves a formal contract, the X is both morally and legally obligated to do *z* (an instance of [c]). Legally, in that X must satisfy the conditions of a contract having the force of law; morally, since an promise to do *z* is presupposed.

It could be argued that in a normal course of events most instances of legal obligation are concurrent with a moral obligation to obey the law; an obligation which is extralegal and normative in basis. That this concurrence does not always obtain would be evident in cases representing (b) and has been the subject of considerable disagreement. Certain laws may enjoin obligations which seem neutral or reprehensible from a moral point of view and in relation to the latter may be thought either to carry no particular obligation beyond that of general obedience to law, or to carry a contrary one. Problems relevant to conflict between a general presumption to obey the law and one's moral obligation not to obey it are manifest in such issues as conscientious refusal and civil disobedience; see Rawls, *A Theory of Justice*, pp. 363–391.

4 Responsibility and the problem of determinism

1 B. F. Skinner, *Beyond Freedom and Dignity* (New York: Alfred A. Knopf, 1971), pp. 17–18.

2 Ibid., pp. 18–19.

3 Ibid., p. 74.

4 Willard Gaylin, "Skinner Redux," *Harper's*, (Oct. 1973), p. 50. This citation has been reprinted with permission of the author.

5 Ibid., p. 50.

6 Skinner, *Beyond Freedom*, p. 157.

7 Gaylin, "Skinner Redux," p. 50.

5 Moral and legal accountability

1 The relationship itself needs further explanation. As mentioned earlier, an agent could be required by law to answer to the government concerning

annual income. Should he refuse or falsify his answer, he might have to answer legally either for violating the law requiring that income be reported, or for violating any of several associated laws requiring veracity, full disclosure and so forth. Accountability in this situation involves a change in the elements to whom and for what he would be answerable. Letting "X is answerable to Y for z" represent the relationship, in the first instance Y would be the government and z, income; in the second, Y would be the judiciary and z, either failure to comply with the law or an illegal act in doing so. Again, to whom and for what X is answerable differs; this difference will be indicated by the notation $Y, Y1$ and $z, z1$.

Since X is accountable to Y for z in one instance and to $Y1$ for $z1$ in another, it may seem necessary to designate X's accountability in a similar fashion, i. e., as "accountability" and "accountability 1", thus indicating two distinct relationships. This procedure is questionable because while X's relationships to Y and $Y1$ are different, they are not independent. Being answerable to $Y1$ is contingent either on X's failure to answer Y or on an illegal or unsatisfactory performance regarding z. In either case, the second accountability relationship becomes operative due to and only after some difficulty with the first.

Second if being answerable to Y for z means essentially that X is "subject to" answering Y, then the accountability relationship between X and $Y1$ is presupposed; for, as noted, the degree to which X is *subject to* answering Y is a function of the degree to which X is unfree under law requiring him to do so, and X's relationship to $Y1$ is a condition of that unfreedom. Thus, the possibility of being answerable to $Y1$ is presupposed by the notion of being "subject to" in the accountability relationship between X and Y. For this reason it has been assumed that X's accountability to Y extends to include his accountability to the law which supports this relationship.

2   S. I. Benn and R. S. Peters, "Freedom as a Political Ideal," is *The Principles of Political Thought* (New York: The Free Press, 1965), pp. 247–271.

3   In summary, an instance of moral obligation formally implies moral grounds on the basis of which one may justifiably say that it exists; it does not imply, formally, that X is subject to satisfying what it requires, nor actually, that X will satisfy its requirements. An instance of legal obligation formally implies that a law exists defining the conditions of its occurrence, and that X is subject to doing whatever it enjoins to the extent that X is unfree under the law and its enforcement; it does not imply, actually, that X always will be subject to doing what it enjoins, nor that X will satisfy its requirements on any particular occasion.

6 The accountability and moral development of students

1   There are exceptions, of course. Because of the death of a parent or for other reasons, some students are forced into responsibilities not unlike those

common to many adults. They may have to work to provide for their family, be responsible for raising siblings and so forth.

2 L. Kohlberg, "Moral Stages and Moralization: The Cognitive-Developmental Approach," in T. Lickona, ed., *Moral Development and Behavior: Theory, Research, and Social Issues,* (New York: Holt, Rinehart and Winston, 1976), pp. 31–53.

3 L. Kohlberg, "Education for Justice: A Modern Statement of the Platonic View," in T. Sizer ed., *Moral Education,* (Cambridge, Mass: Harvard University Press, 1970), pp. 76–77.

4 L. Kohlberg et al., *Assessing Moral Development* (Cambridge, Mass.: Center for Moral Education, Harvard University, 1977); L. Kohlberg, "Stage and Sequence: The Cognitive-Developmental Approach to Socialization, in D. Goslin, ed., *Handbook of Socialization Theory and Research,* (Chicago: Rand McNally, 1969), pp. 347–480.

5 L. Kohlberg, "Stages of Moral Development as a Basis for Moral Education," in C. Beck and E. Sullivan, eds., *Moral Education* (Toronto: University of Toronto Press, 1970).

6 L. Kohlberg, P. Scharf, and J. Hickey, "The Justice Structure of the Prison: A Theory and an Intervention," *The Prison Journal* 61 (Autumn–Winter 1972), pp. 3–14.

7 Teacher accountability: Three basic issues

1 James S. Coleman et al., *Equality of Educational Opportunity* (Washington, D. C.; U. S. Government Printing Office, 1966).

2 Christopher Jencks, "A Reappraisal of the Most Controversial Educational Document of Our Time," *New York Times Magazine,* Aug. 10, 1969.

3 Charles Silberman, *Crisis in the Classroom* (New York: Vintage, 1971), p. 71.

4 Ibid. Silberman's study has been criticized on the grounds that it involves a number of procedural and methodological weaknesses. However, subsequent analysis tends to support its general findings concerning the significance of extraschool influences on student achievement. For an interesting discussion of these problems, see Frederick Mosteller and Daniel P. Moynihan, eds., *On Equality of Educational Opportunity* (New York: Vintage, 1972). The latter work contains several papers resulting from a Harvard University faculty seminar on the Coleman report.

5 "Book Burning," *The New York Times,* Nov. 17, 1974.

6 "Police, Escorting a School Bus, Fired upon in Textbook Dispute," *The New York Times,* Nov. 14, 1974, p. 12.

7 Silberman, *Crisis,* p. 11.

8 Arthur H. Rice, "Good Teachers Stand to Benefit from Accountability Plans," *Nation's Schools* 86 (Dec. 1970), p. 16.

9 A conclusion of the Holmes Group Report. See *Tomorrow's Teachers: A Report of the Holmes Group* (East Lansing, Mich.: The Holmes Group, 1986), pp. 27–40, 67–68.

Bibliography

Books

Annual Editions: Readings in Education. Guilford, Conn.: Dushkin. 1973.

Benn, S. I., and R. S. Peters, *The Principles of Political Thought.* New York: The Free Press. 1965.

Brandt, Richard B. *Ethical Theory.* Englewood Cliffs: Prentice-Hall. 1963.

Coleman, James S., *et al. Equality of Educational Opportunity.* Washington D. C.: U. S. Government Printing Office. 1966.

Cornford, Francis MacDonald, trans. *The Republic of Plato.* Oxford: Oxford University Press. 1965.

Cruickshank, William M. *Education of Exceptional Children and Youth.* Englewood Cliffs: Prentice-Hall. 1967.

Frankena, William K. *Ethics.* Englewood Cliffs: Prentice Hall. 1963.

Hare, R. M. *Freedom and Reason.* New York: Oxford University Press. 1965.

Kerr, Clark. *The Uses of the University.* New York: Harper and Row. 1963.

Kohlberg, L. "Stage and Sequence: The Cognitive-Developmental Approach to Socialization." In D. Goslin, ed. *Handbook of Socialization Theory and Research.* Chicago: Rand McNally. 1969.

_____"Stages of Moral Development as a Basis for Moral Education." In C. Beck and E. Sullivan, eds. *Moral Education.* Toronto: University of Toronto Press. 1970.

_____"Education for Justice: A Modern Statement of the Platonic View." In T. Sizer, ed. *Moral Education.* Cambridge: Harvard University Press. 1970.

_____"Moral Stages and Moralization: The Cognitive-Developmental Approach." In T. Lickona, ed. *Moral Development and Behavior: Theory, Research, and Social Issues.* New York: Holt, Rinehart and Winston. 1976.

Lessinger, Leon. *Every Kid a Winner: Accountability in Education.* New York: Simon and Schuster. 1970.

Lessinger, Leon and Ralph W. Tyler. *Accountability in Education.* Worthington: Charles A. Jones Publishing Company. 1971.

Miller, Merle. *Plain Speaking: An Oral Biography of Harry S. Truman.* Berkley. 1974.

Mosteller, Frederick and Daniel P. Moynihan, eds. *On Equality of Educational Opportunity.* New York: Random House. 1972.

Onions, C.T., ed. *The Oxford Universal Dictionary on Historical Principles.* Oxford: Oxford University Press, 1955.

Peters, R.S. *Ethics and Education.* Atlanta: Scott, Foresman. 1967.

Postman, Neil and Charles Weingartner. *Teaching as a Subversive Activity.* New York: Delacorte Press, 1969.

Proxmire, William. *Report From Wasteland: America's Military-Industrial Complex.* New York: Praeger. 1970.

Rawls, John. *A theory of Justice.* Cambridge: Harvard University Press. 1971.

Ross, W. D. *The Right and the Good.* Oxford: Clarendon Press, 1930.

Scheffler, Israel. *Reason and Teaching.* New York: Bobbs-Merrill. 1973.

Sciara, Frank J., and Richard K. Jantz. *Accountability in American Education.*Boston: Allyn and Bacon. 1972.

Silberman, Charles E. *Crisis in the Classroom.* New York: Vintage. 1971.

Tomorrow's Teachers: A Report of the Holmes Group. East Lansing, Mich.: The Holmes Group. 1986.

Webster's Seventh New Collegiate Dictionary. Springfield, Mass.: Merriam. 1965.

Wittgenstein, Ludwig. *Philosophical Investigations.* Translated by G. E. M. Anscombe. New York: Macmillan. 1968.

Wynne, Edward. *The Politics of School Accountability.* Berkeley, Calif.: Mc-Cutchan. 1972.

Journals

Albert, James G. "Wanted: Experiment in Reducing the Cost of Education." *Phi Delta Kappan* 55, no. 7 (March 1974), pp. 444–445.

"Cost of Education Index: 1971–72." *School Management* 16 (Jan. 1972), pp. 21–57.

Cunningham, Luvern L. "Our Accountability Problems." *Theory into Practice* 8 (October. 1969), pp. 285–292.

Davies, Donald. "The Relevance of Accountability." *Journal of Teacher Education* 21 (Spring 1970), pp. 127–133.

Kohlberg, Lawrence, and Rochelle Mayer. "Development as the Aim of Education." *Harvard Educational Review* 42 no. 4 (Nov. 1972), pp. 440–494.

Kohlberg, L., P. Scharf, and J. Hickey. "The Justice Structure of the Prison: A Theory and an Intervention." *The Prison Journal* 61, no. 2 (Autumn-Winter 1972), pp. 3–14.

Mecklenburger, James, and John Wilson. "The Performance Contract in Gary." *Phi Delta Kappan* 52 (March 9, 1971), pp. 406–411.

Milliken, William G. "Making the School System Accountable." *Compact* 4 (Oct. 1970), pp. 17–18.

Pincoffs, Edmund L. "Educational Accountability." *Studies in Philosophy and Education* 8 (Fall 1973), pp. 131–145.

Rice, Arthur H. "Good Teachers Stand to Benefit from Accountability Plans." *Nation's Schools* 86 (December 1970), p. 16.

Other

The Accountability Notebook. Center for Instructional Research and Curriculum Evaluation (CIRCE), University of Illinois.

"Book Burning." *New York Times,* Nov. 17, 1974.

"Clothing." *New York Times,* July 28, 1973.

Lessinger, Leon. *Accountability in Education.* National Committee in Support of the Public Schools. 1970.

Levin, Henry M. *A Conceptual Framework for Accountability in Education.* Stanford University Occasional Paper 72–10. 1972.

Jencks, Christopher. "A Reprisal of the Most Controversial Educational Document of Our Time." *New York Times Magazine,* Aug. 10, 1969.

Kohlberg, L., et al. *Assessing Moral Development.* Cambridge, Mass.: Center for Moral Education, Harvard University. 1977.

Mecklenberger, James A., and John A. Wilson. "Learning C. O. D.: Can the Schools Buy Success?" *Saturday Review,* Sept. 18, 1971.

"Police, Escorting a School Bus, Fired upon the Textbook Dispute." *New York Times,* Nov. 14, 1974.

Related readings

Allen, J. E., Jr. "Competence for All as the Goal for Secondary Education." *National Association of Secondary School Principals Bulletin* 54 (May 1970), pp. 9–17.

"American Public Ill-Informed about Education." *Nation's Schools* 84 (Oct. 1969), p. 16.

Austin, G. R. "Educational Accountability: Hallmark of the 1970's." *Science Teacher* 38 (April 1971), pp. 26–128.

Bain, Helen. "Self-Governance Must Come First, Then Accountability." *Phi Delta Kappan* 51 (April 1970), pp. 413.

Barber, W. R. "Accountability, Bane or Boon?" *School and Community* 57 (April 1971), pp. 14–15.

Benne, K. D. "Authority in Education." *Harvard Educational Review* 40 (Aug. 1970), pp. 385–410

Brick, M. "support for Public Education? Who's Kidding Who?" *National Elementary Principal.* 49 (May 1970), pp. 64–66.

Carline, D. E. "Why Do You Teach? Or How Accountable Are You?" *Journal of Reading,* March 1971, pp. 385–386.

Cass, J. "Accountable to Whom? For What?" *Saturday Review* 54 (March 20, 1970), p. 41.

Cook, Constance, "Sharing the Duty to Account." *Compact* 4 (Oct. 1970), pp. 24–25.

Gillis, James. "Performance Contracting for Public Schools." *Educational Technology,* May 1969, pp. 17–20.

Green, Edith. "The Business of Education." *Nation's Schools* 86 (Dec. 1970), pp. 40–45.

Harlacher, E. L., and E. Roberts. "Accountability for Student Learning." *Junior College Journal* 41 (March 1971), pp. 26–30.

Leight, Robert L., ed. *Philosophers Speak on Accountability in Education.* Danville, Ill.: Interstate Printers and Publishers. 1973.

Lessinger, Leon. "Accountability and Curriculum Reform." *Educational Technology* 10 (May 1970), pp. 56–57.

_____"Accountability for Results: A Basic Challenge for America's Schools." *American Education* 5 (June 1969), pp. 2–4.

_____"Powerful Notion of Accountability in Education." *Journal of Secondary Education* 45 (Dec. 1970), pp. 339–347.

Lieberman, M. "An Overview of Accountability." *Phi Delta Kappan* 52 (Dec. 1970), pp. 194–195.

McLenon, T. B., et al. "Can Parents Demand Accountability?" *Instructor* 80 (Aug. 1970), p. 47.

Nelson, F. B. "Some Reflections on Quality Education and Responsibility." *Education Horizons,* special issue, June 1970, pp. 9–14.

Nyquist, Ewald B. "Measuring Purpose and Effectiveness." *Compact* 4 (Oct. 1970), pp. 21–22.

Opinion Poll. "How Education Groups View Contracting." *Nation's Schools* 85 (June 1970), pp. 31–33.

Opinion Poll. "Large Majority Favors Teacher Accountability." *Nation's Schools* 86 (Dec. 1970), p. 33.

"Performance Contracting." *Nation's Schools* 86 (Oct. 1970), pp. 85–86ff.

"Performance Contracting as Catalyst for Reform." *Education Technology* 9 (Aug. 1969), pp. 5–9.

"Performance Contracts Popular but Evaluation Procedures Questionable." *Educational Product Report* 4 (Dec. 1970), pp. 2–4.

"Performance Contracting: Why the Gary School Board Bought It." *American School Board Journal* 158 (Jan. 1971), pp. 19–21.

"PPBS and Assessment: Where Trouble Could Erupt." *Nation's Schools* 83 (June 1969), p. 8.

Rogers, David. "The Failure of Inner City Schools: A Crisis of Management and Service Delivery." *Educational Technology* 10 (Sept. 1970), pp. 27–32. Stocker, J., and D. F. Wilson. "Accountability and the Classroom Teacher." *Today's Education* 60 (March 1971), pp. 41–56.

"What the Public Thinks about the Public Schools: Results of the 1970 Survey." *Education Digest* 36 (Dec. 1970), pp. 1–4.

Williams, L. "Governance Is Integral to Accountability." *Today's Education* 60 (April 1971), pp. 59–60.

Index

DATE DUE

JE 30 '90 SE 01 '90		
AP 29 '92		
AUG 0 8 2000		
ILL		
1571 2026		WITHDRAWN
2/15/06		